Crossing Borders
Hebrew Manuscripts as a Meeting-place of Cultures

CROSSING BORDERS

*Hebrew Manuscripts
as a
Meeting-place of Cultures*

Edited by
Piet van Boxel and Sabine Arndt

Bodleian Library
UNIVERSITY OF OXFORD

First published in 2009 by the Bodleian Library
Broad Street
Oxford OX1 3BG

www.bodleianbookshop.co.uk

ISBN 13: 978 1 85124 313 6

Designed by Dot Little
Printed and bound by Nuffield Press
British Library Catalogue in Publishing Data
A CIP record of this publication is available from the British Library

Contents

Foreword

Sarah Thomas

The history of the Bodleian Library goes back to 1598, when Thomas Bodley (1545–1613) embarked upon a project to restore the old University Library, built to house the gift of books from Humfrey, Duke of Gloucester in the fifteenth century, which in a radical action to purge the English Church of all traces of Roman Catholicism, including superstitious books, had been ransacked some fifty years earlier. At his expense the old library, of which even the bookshelves and desks had been sold, was refurnished to house a new collection of about 2,500 books, some of them given by Bodley himself. In 1605 the first printed catalogue was published, which included works of an explicit Catholic nature and 58 Hebrew titles.

Thomas Bodley's enthusiasm for Hebrew goes back to his early education in the bastion of Protestantism, Geneva. But combined with his knowledge of Latin and his passion for Greek, his Hebrew training made him into a *vir trilinguis.* As a genuine humanist and a Christian Hebraist Thomas Bodley was not bound by ideological borders and rose above the religious confrontation of conflicting denominations, which previously had led to the pillage of Duke Humfrey's library.

At the time of the opening of the library there was only one Arabic manuscript, a Qur'an which had been donated in 1601, and during the first decade only a few Arabic manuscripts were acquired, despite great efforts of the founder.

It was only in the years after Sir Thomas Bodley's death that the holdings were further enriched when Archbishop Laud donated some 250 manuscripts in Oriental languages to the library, of which 147 were in Arabic and 47 in Hebrew. Through this and later acquisitions, which made Oxford a major centre for Oriental studies and the Oriental collections a worthy counterpart of the Western holdings of the Library, Thomas Bodley's dream came true.

'Crossing borders' could well have been the motto of the founder of the Bodleian Library. His unfettered understanding of what constitutes a library laid the foundation for cross-cultural reading and created the context and ambiance in which the material book can not only be comprehended, but also appreciated.

This collection of essays entitled *Crossing Borders: Hebrew Manuscripts as a Meeting-place of Cultures* which accompanies an exhibition of some exquisite items from the Arabic, Latin and Hebrew holdings of the Bodleian Library, embodies this kind of reading. It reflects recent developments in Oxford of the study of the book, in which Oriental and Western collections together play an important part.

I would like to thank Dr Piet van Boxel, Curator of Hebrew and Jewish Collections at the Bodleian Library and Librarian of the Centre for Hebrew and Jewish Studies at Yarnton, who has curated the exhibition and edited this volume of essays together with Sabine Arndt, as well as the individual contributors to the volume. The Bodleian Library is indebted to the Rothschild Foundation, to the Ronald S. Cohen Charitable Trust, the Congregation of the Sisters of Sion, the Oxford Centre for Hebrew and Jewish Studies and the Hebrew Unit of the Oriental Faculty for their financial support towards the exhibition and publication.

בראשית

בָּרָא אֱלֹהִים אֵת הַשָּׁמַיִם וְאֵת הָאָרֶץ ׃ וְהָאָרֶץ הָיְתָה תֹהוּ וָבֹהוּ
וְחֹשֶׁךְ עַל־פְּנֵי תְהוֹם וְרוּחַ אֱלֹהִים מְרַחֶפֶת עַל־פְּנֵי הַמָּיִם ׃ וַיֹּאמֶר
אֱלֹהִים יְהִי אוֹר וַיְהִי־אוֹר ׃ וַיַּרְא אֱלֹהִים אֶת־הָאוֹר כִּי־טוֹב וַיַּבְדֵּל
אֱלֹהִים בֵּין הָאוֹר וּבֵין הַחֹשֶׁךְ ׃ וַיִּקְרָא אֱלֹהִים לָאוֹר יוֹם וְלַחֹשֶׁךְ קָרָא
לָיְלָה וַיְהִי־עֶרֶב וַיְהִי־בֹקֶר יוֹם אֶחָד ׃

וַיֹּאמֶר אֱלֹהִים יְהִי רָקִיעַ בְּתוֹךְ הַמָּיִם וִיהִי מַבְדִּיל בֵּין מַיִם לָמָיִם ׃
וַיַּעַשׂ אֱלֹהִים אֶת־הָרָקִיעַ וַיַּבְדֵּל בֵּין הַמַּיִם אֲשֶׁר מִתַּחַת לָרָקִיעַ וּבֵין
הַמַּיִם אֲשֶׁר מֵעַל לָרָקִיעַ וַיְהִי־כֵן ׃ וַיִּקְרָא אֱלֹהִים לָרָקִיעַ שָׁמַיִם וַיְהִי־
עֶרֶב וַיְהִי־בֹקֶר יוֹם שֵׁנִי ׃

וַיֹּאמֶר אֱלֹהִים יִקָּווּ הַמַּיִם מִתַּחַת הַשָּׁמַיִם אֶל־מָקוֹם אֶחָד וְתֵרָאֶה
הַיַּבָּשָׁה וַיְהִי־כֵן ׃ וַיִּקְרָא אֱלֹהִים לַיַּבָּשָׁה אֶרֶץ וּלְמִקְוֵה הַמַּיִם קָרָא
יַמִּים וַיַּרְא אֱלֹהִים כִּי־טוֹב ׃ וַיֹּאמֶר אֱלֹהִים תַּדְשֵׁא הָאָרֶץ דֶּשֶׁא עֵשֶׂב

Introduction

Piet van Boxel

In the introduction to his pioneering monograph The Order of Books, Roger Chartier proposes 'to initiate more general reflection on the reciprocal relations between the two meanings that we spontaneously give to the term "culture". The first designates the works and the acts that lend themselves to aesthetic or intellectual appreciation in any given society; the second aims at ordinary, banal practices that express the way in which a community – on any scale – experiences and conceives of its relationship with the world, with others, and with itself'.[1] It is the printed book, its authors, producers and readers that constitute the focus of Chartier's reflections. But his words could just as well have been written in relation to manuscripts, scribes and owners. We should not forget that there is an intimate relationship between the making of manuscripts and printed books – after all, the books printed from the invention of the art of typography in the 1450s to the end of the fifteenth century, known as incunabula, were intentionally made to look like manuscripts (figure 1). Chartier's twofold meaning of culture may therefore be adopted as an apposite way of reflecting upon the Hebrew manuscript as a meeting-place of cultures – for they, too, contain works of 'intellectual appreciation' and 'ordinary practices' of production.

It should be noted that Chartier places both meanings of culture in the context of 'any given society'. In the case of the Jews of medieval Europe this means a large variety of societies to which they belonged. But to what extent did owners and producers of Hebrew manuscripts share their aesthetic and intellectual appreciation with the society in which they lived? Equally it should be asked to what degree the practice of Jewish book production reflects a relationship with the non-Jewish world.

Figure 1
The Holkham Bible, printed in Naples in 1491 or 1492 by Joshua Solomon Soncino, lavishly illuminated like a manuscript. Oxford, Bodleian Library, Holkham c. 1.

אמר שמואל

יהודה קדם

כל מהיותי מכב בעניני השיאינ טבבו טבא במטעוב ההטבתבה הצב הכוה וצבר בבר מזה ובבר
מזה ובל צבר ידיעת הטבוו המוטבתב ממכנ מוזכני שמושיו והבבת דבי הסט נעטבני
מהיימיו ובבל צבר ידיעת הטבוו המוטבתב זכו ובבבורטיו סעיטני צמיביי נחבצין מחזיממב
זה מטבו שההטבתבה היי מעטבה זחר   לבב מעטה יש זבבבסבבת בברצ וטבות וטהבעטונדו
נצו ימטבו מזמר מחב   ונהס הפוטבע והזומר והטברה וההטבבות וגהטבה הפלטבוזות צביר
טובבה צ בביר במטבר יעטבה זגזה בבבו הב בתגבגבר מטצנ יטהזה זמו מצ המעטביר יטבגב
מצצוזתו הצ הטבמי והוז הפוטבע והזזבבס והבבוונת נהבבוונת נבטב מזה עלצביר צ הבויזב בבבוט
טהס התחמר צוז יטעטה הבוטה צנרתבבתבת נזמגנס הצו עביר בעטבונדנו וצגתב צ לבבר זיבס ימבצן
בהצ לצזבבבבר והעטביס טבביר צבו לבבבני עני יצהבבנבה מטבגה בבדונו זיו יבעב ההבבבנו גבמלבבט
בבבב הטבת בגהצ טבנו בב נטבהטבבנו בב הנה צו בבבבנ טבבנב נבל צצונ ת הבבד צבו ההעטבב

In recent years there has been a proliferation of studies – palaeo-graphical, codicological and art-historical – of the Hebrew material text, as well as on the non-Jewish context in which Hebrew book production took place. Not only the investigation of literary works but also scrutiny of the actual making of Hebrew manuscripts in the Jewish Diaspora has contributed to historical reconstruction of Jewish life in the Middle Ages. This multifaceted study of the Hebrew manuscript goes beyond the textual information that it contains and takes into account material elements such as paper and parchment, ink and script, layout and the composition of the codex.[2] These non-textual components of the Hebrew codex bear distinctive features of the locality in which they were produced. In addition, the study of Hebrew manuscript illustrations and illuminations in their geocultural context yields precious information about medieval Jews and their environment. As recent comparative research has shown, Jewish scribes not infrequently turned to Christian workshops for the illustration of their manuscripts. It should not come as a surprise that such manuscripts reflect the artistic features and cultural characteristics of those ateliers and occasionally even contain explicit Christian motifs. What is striking is that the manuscripts illuminated by Jewish artists also reflect local cultural practices.[3] They display coexistence, cultural affinity as well as practical cooperation between Jews and their non-Jewish neighbours.

It must be borne in mind, however, that not all the constituent elements that make up any particular manuscript originate in one and the same place. Often, probably due to economic circumstances, scribes moved from one region or even one country to another. A manuscript in Sephardic script, for example, does not necessarily mean that it was produced in Spain. Not only scribes travelled, but also pictorial models were imported and found their way to new environments far from their place of origin. Thus Islamic decorative patterns continued to be used by Jewish illuminators who lived in Christian Spain long after Muslim domination had come to an end (figure 2).

The reconstruction of local Jewish history in the Middle Ages should therefore not be based upon one single material source. From the accumulative evidence provided by various elements of the material text we can establish the provenance of a manuscript, whilst elements contradicting the *couleur locale* of a Hebrew codex may shed light on cultural interaction in the Diaspora.

Finally, the study of the material text enhances our understanding of its contents, and enables us to localize the intellectual exchange and transmission of knowledge between Jews, Muslims and Christians. Establishing the provenance of a Hebrew manuscript helps us pinpoint the nature of the intellectual interaction between communities and individuals, thus contributing to a more nuanced account of Jewish life in the Middle Ages.

The Bodleian Library holds one of the finest collections of Hebrew manuscripts. The earliest manuscript accessions in Hebrew were received in 1601, and in the first catalogue of the library produced by the founder Sir Thomas Bodley (1545–1613), who was himself a Hebraist of some distinction, we find fifty-eight books with titles in Hebrew script.[4] After Bodley's death, the Library continued to enrich the Hebrew holdings. In 1692 it purchased the collections of Robert Huntington and Edward Pococke, the Regius Professor of Hebrew. Among the 212 manuscripts in the Huntington collection is the *Mishneh Torah* of Moses Maimonides (1137/8–1204) bearing the signature of this most illustrious Jewish authority (MS. Huntington 80). The acquisition in 1817 of the manuscript collection which had once belonged to the Venetian Jesuit Matteo Luigi Canonici represents the largest single purchase ever made by the Library – the collection contains over 110 valuable Hebrew manuscripts, the majority of which are written on vellum. In 1829 the Bodleian Library bought the Oppenheimer Collection, which has been described as the most important and magnificent Hebraica collection accumulated by any private collector. Rabbi David ben Abraham Oppenheimer (1664–1736) was the Chief Rabbi of Prague, and during his lifetime he amassed 780 manuscripts and 4,220 printed books in Hebrew, Yiddish and Aramaic – many of which are the only surviving copies. Further significant collections of Hebrew manuscripts were added in 1848 and again in 1890. In 1848 the Library purchased the library of Heimann Joseph Michael, which numbered 862 volumes, containing nearly 1,300 separate works. And it was in the 1890s that the Library acquired a collection of Hebrew manuscripts of major international importance with the purchase of 5,000 valuable fragments from the so-called Cairo Genizah, the depository of worn-out and discarded Hebrew books and documents discovered at the end of the nineteenth century in a synagogue in Old Cairo.

From the Bodleian's treasure-trove a small number of Hebrew manuscripts will now come to centre stage. *Crossing Borders: Hebrew Manuscripts as a Meeting-place of Cultures* will tell their story and thus, also, that of the intellectual transmission, cultural exchange and practical cooperation, social interaction and religious toleration between Jews and non-Jews in the Muslim and the Christian worlds during the late Middle Ages. Practical cooperation comes to light in the use of a specific book form – the codex – introduced by Christians as early as the second century, though only, so it seems, with some hesitation, accepted by Jews as late as the ninth century. Regional similarities between Jews and non-Jews in writing, which resulted in various distinctive types of Hebrew script, point to a certain degree of integration and social interaction on a local level. The role of Jews in the transmission of culture and science in medieval Europe comes to the fore in Hebrew translations and adaptations of material which had only been available in Arabic. Illustrations and illuminations of Jewish prayer books produced in Christian workshops attest to a shared culture, and the use by Christians of Jewish tradition made accessible in Hebrew manuscripts reveal cultural and religious exchange.

Through a comparison of Hebrew codices with their Arabic, Latin and other western counterparts a history of culture will emerge, in relation to three major geographical areas: Spain, Italy and northern Europe. It is in these three regions that Jewish communities developed distinctive features, which can only be understood in relation to the cultural characteristics of the wider society. To Hebrew codices we may apply the words of the late Leonard Boyle, the Oxonian Latin palaeographer and former Prefect of the Vatican library, who in his *Medieval Latin Palaeography* stated, 'Writing did not take place in a vacuum, but is a reflection of various cultures and propensities of various times and it provides a window on the mentality, preoccupations and tastes of the people who were responsible for it in its variegated forms.'[5]

NOTES

1.   R. Chartier, *The Order of Books*, trans. L.G. Cochrane (Stanford, 1994), ix.
2.   See the pioneering contributions of Malachi Beit-Arié to the field of Hebrew codicology such as *Hebrew Codicology: Tentative Typology of Technical Practices Employed in Hebrew Dated Medieval Manuscripts* (Jerusalem, 1981); *The Makings of the Medieval Hebrew Book: Studies in Palaeography and Codicology* (Jerusalem, 1993); *Hebrew Manuscripts of East and West: Towards a Comparative Codicology* (London, 1993); *Unveiled Faces of Medieval Hebrew Books: The Evolution of Manuscript Production – Progression or Regression?* (Jerusalem, 2003).
3.   See e.g. B. Narkiss, A. Cohen-Mushlin and A. Tcherikover, *Hebrew Illuminated Manuscripts in the British Isles: A catalogue raisonné*. Vol. 1 (Jerusalem and London, 1982); T. and M. Metzger, *Jewish Life in the Middle Age: Illuminated Hebrew Manuscripts of the Thirteenth to the Sixteenth Centuries* (New York, 1982); G. Sed-Rajna, *Le Mahzor enluminé. Les voies de formation d'un programme iconographique* (Leiden, 1983); Y. Zirlin, 'Celui qui se cache derrière l'image: colophons des enlumineurs dans les manuscrits hebraïques mediévaux', *Revue des études juives* 155 (1996), 33–53; K. Kogman-Appel, *Jewish Book Art between Islam and Christianity: The Decoration of Hebrew Bibles from Spain* (Leiden, 2004); E. Frojmovic, 'Jewish Scribes and Christian Illuminators: Interstertial Encounters and Cultural Negotiation', in K. Kogman-Appel and M. Meyer, eds, *Between Judaism and Christianity: Art Historical Essays in Honor of Elisheva (Elisabeth) Revel-Neher* (Leiden, 2008) 281–305.
4.   *Catalogus Librorum Bibliothecae Publicae quam vir ornatissimus Thomas Bodleius Eques Auratus in Academia Oxoniensi nuper instituit...* (Oxford, Joseph Barnes, 1605).
5.   L. Boyle, *Medieval Latin Palaeography: A Bibliographical Introduction* (Toronto and London, 1984), p.xii.

CHAPTER 1

From Roll to Codex:
A Christian Initiative

Anthony Grafton

The most revolutionary invention in the history of the book is prob-ably the codex. In contrast to the roll – the ordinary book form at the beginning of the Common Era – the leaves of the codex, usually parchment, could be used on both sides, which reduced the size of the codex by half as compared to the roll, making it easier to carry and to store. Despite some attempts in the first century CE to produce books in codex form, the roll remained the dominant form of the book until the third century. The early adaptors of the codex were the Christians, who made it the vehicle for spreading the Christian message. Well known are the famous biblical codices such as the Codex Sinaiticus and the Codex Vaticanus, which contain the Old and the New Testament in Greek, the language of the Christian Scriptures. Both from the fourth century, the Codex Sinaiticus, which derives its name from the place where it was discovered, St Catherine's Monastery on Mount Sinai, and the Codex Vaticanus, so called because it is considered the most famous manuscript in the possession of the Vatican Library, are prime examples of Christian book production in codex form. Together with the Codex Alexandrinus from *c.* 400, so named because it was brought to Europe from Alexandria and had been the property of the patriarch of that see, they not only played an important part in developing the textual criticism of the Bible, particularly of the New Testament, but are also of extreme impor-tance for the history of the book. The subsequent slow and gradual change in book making from the book roll towards the codex as the medium of non-Christian texts seems to coincide with the expansion of Christianity in the Roman Empire.

The establishment of Christianity as the official religion of the Empire in the fourth century consolidated the position of the codex as the favourite book form. Hebrew book production, however, does not seem to follow this trend. The earliest reference to the codex form in Jewish literature does not date before the end of the eighth or the beginning of the ninth century. From the fragmentary evidence we have of book production by Greek-speaking Jews no conclusion can be drawn as to whether they used the codex as book form. While adhering to the roll book, the late adoption of the codex by the Jews may well reflect an effective means of dissociating themselves from the Christians, who first used the codex for disseminating the New Testament and the translation of the Old Testament. In addition they produced codices of those writers who were considered to be spokesmen of Christian tradition, in particular with regard to the interpretation of Scripture. Their writings were an essential tool for understanding the Christian message. No two of them proved more influential over the centuries than Philo of Alexandria (c. 15 BCE–50 CE) and Eusebius of Caesarea (c. 263–339). Works of both have been preserved in codex form. Philo, a Jew of noble descent, followed Jewish law with passion and precision, and treated the Hebrew Bible as both the source and the criterion of truth in all realms of thought. Eusebius, a Christian of unknown origins, upheld the unique value of the New Testament with equal passion, and devoted much of his life and work to making the Christian Bible accessible and understand-able. They seem very different. Yet in some ways the two men devoted themselves to parallel enterprises, and both left lasting legacies to the Christian church.

Both Philo and Eusebius held that in order to attain a correct interpretation of the Bible, Jewish or Christian, the scholar needed to master the most up-to-date intellectual tools – including those forged outside their own traditions. Philo applied the tools of philosophy to the interpretation of the Old Testament. He offered an interpreta-tion of the Creation that drew on Greek cosmology and one of the Pentateuch that drew on Greek ethics, and by doing so he founded a tradition of exegesis that would – in Christian hands – become central to Christianity (figure 3). Eusebius did much the same, not only in his own biblical commentaries, but also in the *Preparation for the Gospel*, in which he argued that the best pagan thinkers had been granted glimpses of the truth reserved, before the coming of Jesus, to the Jews. In addition to philosophy, however, Eusebius drew on the tools of philology. Using techniques developed by Origen (185–254) and by his own teacher Pamphilus (latter half of the third century), he set out to establish the most accurate possible text of the Bible in Greek, to connect the people, events and places it mentioned with those recorded by pagan historians, and to re-create the history of the Christian church.

Both Philo and Eusebius achieved great eminence in their own time. Philo represented the Jews of Alexandria, who had suffered much violence from other inhabitants of the city, on an embassy to the emperor Caligula, which he described in detail. Eusebius served the emperor Constantine, the first emperor to accept Christianity as the religion of the Empire, in many ways. He served as bishop of the great see at Caesarea in Palestine, provided Bibles for the churches of Constantine's new capital at Constantinople, and wrote the emperor's life. More important, both of them became vital models for later Christian writers. Many early Christian writers, especially the Alexandrians Clement (*c.* 150–215) and Origen, valued Philo as a great authority on the Scriptures. They applied his methods of literal and allegorical exegesis in their own commentaries.

Eusebius followed Origen – and Philo – in his own work as teacher and commentator on the Bible. He also laid some of the foundations for the immense esteem that Philo enjoyed – more than any other Jewish writer except the historian Josephus – in the Christian tradition.

Figure 3
Philo Judaeus, *Sacrarum Legum Allegoria* (allegorical interpretation of Scripture). Early example of the codex form (third century). Oxford, Bodleian Library, MS. Gr. class. c. 74 (P) / 2.

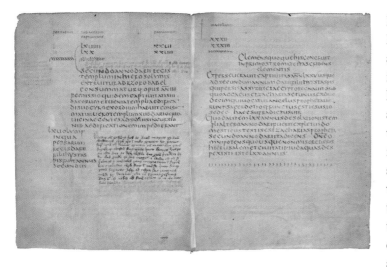

Figure 4
Eusebius' *Chronicle*
translated into Latin
and edited by Jerome.
The oldest manuscript of
the *Chronicle* at present
known (sixth century).
Oxford, Bodleian Library,
MS. Auct. T. 2.26, fols
81v–82r.

In the *Ecclesiastical History* Eusebius quoted Philo's account of a group of ascetics, the *Therapeutae*, whom he identified as Christian ascetics. For Eusebius, Philo's warm appreciation of their renunciation of property and self-indulgence and their devotion to prayer and meditation showed that he himself, though Jewish, had been close to the early Christians, and had sympathized with them: 'And since he describes as accurately as possible the life of our ascetics, it is clear that he not only knew, but that he also approved, while he venerated and extolled, the apostolic men of his time' (Eusebius, *Ecclesiastical History* 2.17.2).

Later Christian writers continued to treat Philo, in varied ways, as both an authority and a valuable source of ideas and methods. Jerome (c. 340–420), for example, agreed with Eusebius that Philo had been a sympathetic witness to the earliest development of Christian monasticism. Others showed more reserve – and more awareness that Philo had belonged to a different religion. Augustine (354–430), by contrast, though he praised Philo's grasp of exegetical principles, noted that as a Jew he had not been able to apply them correctly. He had been right to see the ark as modelled on the human body – but wildly wrong to argue that the opening made in its side corresponded to 'the lower parts of the body, through which urine and excrement are released'. Majority opinion, however, simply assimilated Philo to the Christian tradition and even to the Christian Church. In Byzantine *catenae*, or anthologies of passages relevant to the explication of the Scriptures, texts from Philo were ascribed to 'Philo the Bishop'.

Eusebius, for his part, provided multiple models for Christian scholarship in the centuries after his time. His richly erudite *Ecclesiastical History* became the model for a whole genre of Christian writing, which took its distinctive characteristics – such as its ample provision of whole documents that described the piety of individual Christian martyrs and leaders – as exemplary. His *Chronicle* (figure 4), and his powerful works on the ways in which the best pagan thinkers offered incomplete glimpses of the truth by God, had prepared the way for Christianity, served as vital sources for hundreds of years to come. The manuscripts of the New Testament that he and the scribes who worked for him at Caesarea, with their canon tables laid out to show the reader how the Gospels converged and diverged, became standard not only in the Greek east but in Armenian, Slavonic, Syriac (figure 5) and Latin Bibles (figure 6) as well.

Above all, the community of Christian scholars that Eusebius created at Caesarea and the rich library that he built up there were remembered as models, not only in the learned monastic world that grew up in the Middle Ages, but a millennium and more later, when Protestant and Catholic scholars set out to devise institutions to further Christian scholarship.

Figure 5

The four Gospels in Syriac (probably fifth century). Oxford, Bodleian Library, MS. Dawkins 3, fols 20v–21r.

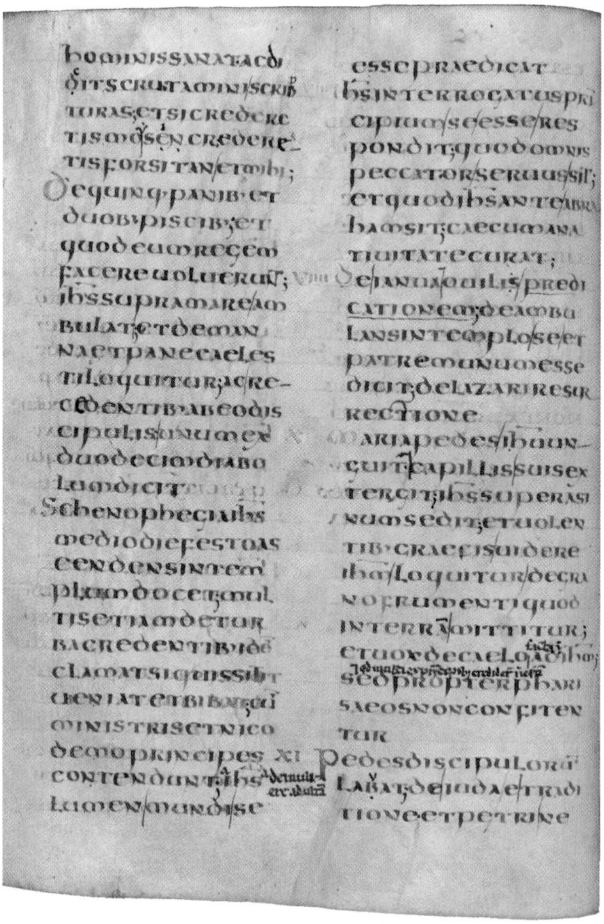

Figure 6

Gospel Book in Latin (Italy, sixth or seventh century). Oxford, Bodleian Library, MS. Auct. D. 2.14, fol. 129v.

Figure 7
Torah scroll (Genesis 32:6
-36:12), fragment from the
Cairo Genizah (probably
thirteenth century).
Oxford, Bodleian Library,
MS. Heb. a. 4, fol. 2r.

The works of both Philo and Eusebius, like those of other early Christian writers together with the Christian Bible, were disseminated throughout the Roman Empire in codex form. It was not until the ninth century that this book form was adapted in Hebrew manuscript production. In synagogues, however, the Torah scroll remains in use today (figure 7).

References

M. Beit-Arié, *Hebrew Manuscripts of East and West: Towards a Comparative Codicology* (The Panizzi Lectures) (London, 1993), 9–11.

A. Grafton and M. Williams, *Christianity and the Transformation of the Book* (Cambridge, Mass., 2006).

C.H. Roberts and T.C. Skeat, *The Birth of the Codex* (London, 1983).

D. Runia, *Philo in Early Christian Literature: A Survey* (Philadelphia, 1993).

CHAPTER 2

The Script and Book Craft in the
Hebrew Medieval Codex

Malachi Beit-Arié

The extraordinary historical circumstances that scattered the Jewish communities around the Mediterranean basin and further to the east, north and west brought them into contact with diversified civilizations, religions and societies. The mobility of individual Jews – either by choice or by economic necessity – and of entire communities – by force – made them agents of cross-cultural contacts and influences. Their manuscripts are, therefore, significant artefacts for studying the history of the handwritten book in all the other civilizations around the Mediterranean, predominantly those of Islam and Christianity. Due to the far-flung territorial dispersion of the Jews, and their adherence to their national script, medieval manuscripts written in Hebrew characters were produced in a territorial range larger than that of their Greek, Latin or even Arabic counterparts. Hebrew handwritten books were manufactured and disseminated within and across all these main and other, more minor, booklore zones. The intricate and complex reality of the Jewish existence in the Middle Ages is reflected in MS. Oxford, Corpus Christi College 133, a daily prayer book in an Ashkenazic (northern European) hand. At the end of the manuscript a creditor recorded in Arabic, written in Hebrew characters, in a cursive Sephardic (Spanish) type of script, payments made to him by English debtors, apparently while a moneylender in England (figure 8).

Hebrew manuscripts shared along with other manuscripts of the codex civilizations – in particularly with the Islamic and Christian booklores – the basic structure of the codex form of the book: the same anatomy, the same materials and therefore similar proportions and formats, a molecular structure of quiring achieved by folding a certain number of bifolia, and the employment of means for ensuring the right sequence of the quires or the bifolia and folios within the

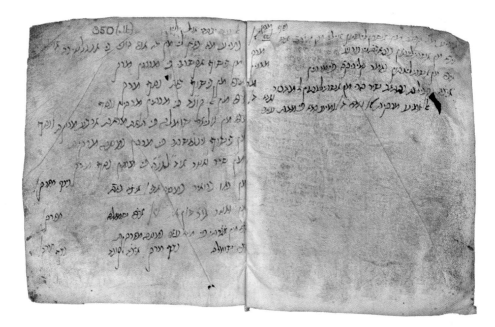

Figure 8
Record of debts in Judeo-
Arabic on the blank pages
of an Ashkenazic prayer
book (*c.* 1200). Oxford,
Corpus Christi College,
MS. 133, fols 349v–350r.

quires, located on the margins. As with Latin, Greek or Arabic, the
designs were planned and the parchment was ruled in preparation for
copying. Scribal practices aimed at an aesthetic and legible presentation of the text, and parts of the manuscripts were decorated and
illuminated in the margins or within the written space.

Moreover, due to the wide dispersion of Hebrew book production,
the similarity between the appearance, writing styles, writing material, technical making and text configuration of the Hebrew codices
and those of the non-Hebrew codices produced in their surrounding
culture is greater than their similarity to Hebrew manuscripts produced in another geocultural region despite their shared script and
texts. Yet the social circumstances of their production, dissemination and consumption were different, particularly from those of the
Christian world.

Until the central Middle Ages Latin handwritten books were
mainly produced in monastic centres, where books were copied in
scriptoria according to ecclesiastical needs and functions or by order
of other monasteries. The books were usually stored, used and studied
in the location where they were made. Later, they were also conceived
and produced in cathedral schools and universities. It was only in
the thirteenth century that Latin manuscript production extended
beyond the monastic and ecclesiastical framework and gradually
handed over to commercial enterprise, mostly centred in ateliers.

The fundamental difference between Hebrew and Latin, Greek and
to some extent Arabic book production stemmed from two cardinal
factors of medieval Jewish life in the East and West: general literacy

and the lack of political power and organization. It is often claimed that – unlike the Christian societies of the West and Byzantium, where literacy was confined to the clergy in monasteries and cathedral schools, then in universities, and in the late Middle Ages reaching also the lay aristocracy, the upper classes and the bourgeois merchants – the majority of Jewish males were literate. The egalitarian system of elementary education, financed and administered by the autonomous Jewish communities, made nearly all male children competent in reading (probably less in writing) Hebrew, acquainted them at least with the basic religious, liturgical and legal texts, and encouraged further advanced education. Lack of political structure and the vast dispersion over different political entities prevented the emergence of centralized Jewish establishments and religious or secular leader-ship, despite communal self-government, internal social and juridical autonomy, and the powerful authority of individual sages.

These two factors affected and moulded book production and text reproduction. General literacy and the lack of centralized political or intellectual establishments shaped the individual and personal nature of Hebrew book production and precluded the standardization of the reproduced texts.

Medieval Hebrew books were not produced, preserved or dissemi-nated by any specific establishment or upon its initiative. They did not emerge from any religious, academic or lay institutional copying centres, nor were they produced by large-scale commercial enter-prises; they were not collected, preserved or made accessible in any public or sectarian institutions, but were privately and individually produced and used. Books were either produced by professional or semi-professional scribes commissioned by private individuals, or were made by the users themselves. The recording and systematic study of almost all extant Hebrew manuscripts with dated colophons indicate that at least half of them were personal user-produced books, copied by educated persons for their own needs, and only half, or probably less than half, were written by hired copyists, who in many cases were not professional scribes. Whereas the institutional and centralized character of Latin book making and text dissemination – whether carried out in, or initiated by, monasteries, cathedral schools, universities or commercial outlets – enabled supervision and control over the propagation of texts and the standardization of versions, no authoritative guidelines or monitoring procedure could have been involved in the private transmission of texts written in Hebrew characters.

The number of surviving medieval books of the Jewish minority is naturally much smaller than that of extant Latin or Arabic ones.

Figure 9
Fragment of the Hebrew
text of the book of
Ecclesiastes (ch. 40)
from the Cairo Genizah.
Oxford, Bodleian Library,
MS. Heb. e. 62, fol. a.

Figure 10 *right*
Rotulus, book roll
preceding the codex form.
Liturgical text from the
Cairo Genizah. Oxford,
Bodleian Library, MS.
Heb. a. 3, fol. 33v.

However, the extant manuscripts probably represent only a small pro-portion of the total Jewish book production, very likely much smaller than the proportion of Latin manuscripts relative to total Latin book production. The loss of the majority of the codices was not the con-sequence of historical conditions alone. Not only were Hebrew books destroyed or abandoned through wanderings, emigrations, persecutions and expulsions, or confiscated and burned in Christian countries; they were above all worn out by use. The discovery of the so-called Cairo Genizah in the Palestinian Synagogue in Fustat (old Cairo) provides us with a tangible sample of the extent of book consumption and literacy among medieval Jews. The bulk of the approximately 200,000, mostly literary, fragments was stored mainly over a period of about 250 years, apparently between 1025 and 1266 and constitutes the remains of some 30,000 books which were used until they were eventually worn out and finally disposed of by one sector of the three Jewish communities in one city alone (figures 9 and 10).

Moreover, the roughly 100,000 extant medieval Hebrew codices and their consolidated scattered fragments represent the output of only the last six centuries of medieval book production. The revo-lutionary codex form of the book, which was adopted and diffused by Christians already in the first centuries of our era and replaced the old roll form in the areas around the Mediterranean from about 300, was employed by the Jews much later, as is attested both by findings and by textual evidence. Between the abundant finds of

Hebrew books from Late Antiquity – the Dead Sea Scrolls from the Qumran caves and the Judean desert of the Hellenistic and early Roman period – and the earliest dated and datable surviving Hebrew codices, there is a gap of some 800 years almost entirely without evidence of the Hebrew book, in either roll or codex form. The late employment of the codex may very well reflect the basically oral nature of the transmission of Hebrew post-Biblical literature.

The earliest extant categorically dated Hebrew codices were written at the beginning of the tenth century, all of them in the Middle East. However, in the structural shaping and artistic design of the copied texts, in their harmonious scripts and shared styles, these earliest manuscripts demonstrate elaborate craftsmanship and regularity, attesting to a long-established tradition of codex design and production, probably from the ninth century onwards. Dated eleventh-century manuscripts have survived from Italy and the Maghreb – present Morocco, Algeria and Tunisia – whilst those produced in the Iberian peninsula, France, Germany, England and Byzantium date from the twelfth century onwards. Until the thirteenth century their number is rather small, particularly outside the Middle East, but thereafter it grows, reaching a peak in the fifteenth century.

Though we do have significant information on the earlier stages of book production and script in the Orient, we lack such knowledge concerning the formation period in the Christian world. This applies to western and central Europe and the Byzantine zone, as well as in North Africa and Muslim Spain. Yet, some 80 per cent of the extant dated manuscripts were produced within the orbit of the Christian world, and only about 20 per cent in the Muslim lands. The development of early handwritten books in Christian territories in the central Middle Ages must have been inspired by the Oriental codex, with book production becoming more developed and elaborate in the late Middle Ages. Diversified techniques, script types, shapes and layouts evolved; transparency of the text, which enabled the users to find their way around it, was enhanced; and decoration and illumination were integrated in the production of books in this period.

Figure 11
Avicenna's *Canon of Medicine* (in Arabic). The title page has five owners' notes in Arabic and one in Hebrew (Egypt, fifteenth century). Oxford, Bodleian Library, MS. Poc. 131, fol. 1r.

Any presentation of the diversified types of the Hebrew script, as well as the making of medieval Hebrew manuscripts, is bound to be related to and shaped by the division of the main civilizations within which Jewish scribes and producers of books were active. The various styles and characteristics of Hebrew handwritten books appear to correspond geographically to the territorial zones of the host religions, cultures and scripts at the time of the formation and crystallization of the Hebrew codex. The affinities between the script and scribal practices employed in Jewish book production and those used in Christian book making in each geocultural area which encompassed Jewish populations may contribute tangible evidence in measuring the degree of acculturation or segregation of the (usually oppressed) Jewish communities contained within Christian societies. They may also help in clarifying the direct symbiotic or indirect osmotic nature of the contacts between Hebrew and Latin scribes.

The distinctive calligraphic and codicological Hebrew traditions cluster in accordance with the three main literate medieval civilizations which flourished around the Mediterranean basin – Islam and its Arabic script, Western Christendom and its Latin script, and Byzantine Christianity and its Greek script. The geographical distribution of those distinctive characteristics corresponds to the geopolitical orbits of Islam, the Latin West and the Greek East in the formative periods of the Hebrew codex. The division of the Jewish

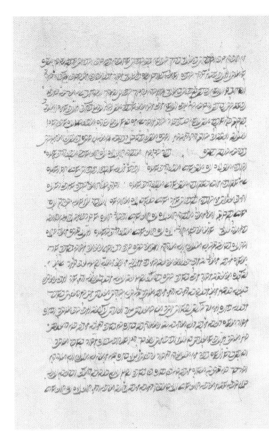

traditions generally persisted until the end of the Middle Ages, notwithstanding major changes in the encompassing geopolitical structure and cultural domination.

Thus Jewish scribal fashions and practices can be grouped into three basic branches. The first is the branch of writing and book making practised in the territories under Muslim rule in the East as well as in the West. Basically this branch shared the same archetypes of script, ductus and the reed as a writing instrument, and were strongly influenced by Arabic calligraphy and book production (figure 11). The second branch includes writing and book production in the territories of Western Europe, which shared the same archetypes of script, ductus and the quill as a writing instrument, and shows a resemblance to the styles and ductus of Latin scripts and Western booklore. The third is the branch of writing and book craft in the areas of the Byzantine Empire before its decline, which seem to have been influenced by Greek script and Byzantine booklore.

Hebrew book script and production of the Islamic domination is clearly divisible into two, namely Eastern and Western, palaeographical and codicological entities. The Eastern Islamic entity – which we

Figure 12 *above left*
Nahmanides, *Torat ha-Adam*, a comprehensive monograph on all the laws concerning death and mourning written in cursive Sephardic script (Spain, 1330). Oxford, Bodleian Library, MS. Mich. 496, fol. 55r.

Figure 13 *above right*
Al-Khushani, *Book of the Judges of Cordoba*. Written in Maghribi script, the Arabic script characteristic of Spain and North Africa (Spain, 1296). MS. Marsh 288, fol. 164r.

Figure 14 *right*
Hebrew Pentateuch
written in Italian semi-
cursive script (Florence,
between 1441–1468).
Oxford, Bodleian Library,
MS. Canon. Or. 22, fol.
111r.

Figure 15 *far right*
Justin's *Epitome of the
'Philippic History' of
Pompeius Trogus*, a
work on ancient history.
Written in humanistic
script, which developed in
Italy in the early fifteenth
century (Milan (?), 1468).
MS. Canon. Class. Lat.
148, fol. 120v.

term Oriental – clusters the Hebrew manuscripts produced in the Near East and Central Asia, within the present boundaries of Iran, Uzbekistan, Iraq, East Turkey, Syria, Lebanon, Israel and the West Bank, Egypt, Yemen and Libya, which at the time when the Hebrew codex was being formed were all contained in one political unit under the Abbasid Caliphate. In general, so far as script is concerned, one can detect differences between the eastern part of the Orient and the western one encompassing Syria, Palestine and Egypt, which may have developed since the late tenth century, when these countries were ruled by the Fatimid dynasty.

The Western Islamic entity of Jewish booklore contains the Iberian peninsula and the Maghreb, which, with the exception of the northern part of Spain, were under Muslim rule, that of the Umayyad Kingdom in Spain, and of the Aghlabids in North Africa, in its formative years. We designate this jewish scribal entity by the term Sephardic (figures 12 and 13). Though the Oriental and Sephardic entities of the Islamic branch have much in common in graphic style and book design, particularly where parchment codices are concerned, each has distinctive types of script and entirely different codicological practices.

The Eastern zone of the Islamic branch is less influenced by Arabic calligraphy, but shows a stronger affinity to Arabic Oriental technical practices, such as the method of processing the writing material, quiring and ruling techniques, and book design and decoration.

Figure 16 *far left*
Dinim (ritual decisions) according to Rabbi Meir of Rothenburg. Written in Ashkenazic Hebrew script, which is clearly influenced by Latin Gothic script (Germany, 1342).Oxford, Bodleian Library, MS. Bodl. Or. 146, fol. 39v.

Figure 17 *left*
Latin missal written in a Gothic script (Bohemia or Moravia, fourteenth century). Oxford, Bodleian Library, MS. Lat. liturg. d. 11, fol. 89v.

The Hebrew booklore encompassed by the territories dominated by Christianity in Western Europe and by the Latin script prevailed in northern France, medieval Germany, England and Italy. This Jewish scribal branch is clearly split into two entities – that of the areas extending north and east from the Alps, and that of Italy. Though certain variations in the style of script and in some codicological features can be discerned between manuscripts produced in France and Germany, and apparently also England, they all cluster into one scribal entity which we term Ashkenazic (Franco-German). The consolidated Ashkenazic scribal entity is probably rooted in the Carolingian period, as its wide sphere corresponds, *grosso modo*, to the territories embraced by the Empire of Charlemagne, which unified Western Christianity at the beginning of the ninth century. England was naturally a later insular extension of this continental tradition. Gradual migration of Jews from Germany eastward extended the Ashkenazic scribal entity to central and Slavic Eastern Europe in the late Middle Ages. Italian manuscripts exhibit distinctive scripts as well as scribal and technical characteristics within the Occidental branch of Hebrew booklore (figures 14 and 15).

The Occidental branch, especially the Ashkenazic entity, displays a clear affinity to styles of Latin script, in particular the Gothic fashions (figures 16 and 17). So far as technical features are concerned the affinities between Hebrew and Latin practices are more complex. Although Ashkenazic manuscripts share with their Latin counterparts

Figure 18
Geo-cultural entities
of Hebrew medieval
manuscripts indicated
on a portolan chart by
Bartholomeo Olives of
Majorca (1575). Oxford,
Bodleian Library, MS.
C2:7 (23).

the same kind of parchment writing material, their ruling techniques do not correspond to those of Latin manuscripts. Where there is correspondence, it is evident that the appearance of such shared practices did not coincide chronologically. The employment of plummet for ruling is illuminating, since it clearly demonstrates that Jewish scribes indeed borrowed this new technology, which was introduced into Latin manuscripts as early as the eleventh century, but only after a significant lapse of time. That Jewish scribes followed the Latin ones is evident not only from the very lateness of the use of the plummet, but from literary sources which show that the new technique had been well known among Jews as early as the twelfth century, but was rejected because of halakhic considerations. The subsequent emergence of the literary genre of biblical texts surrounded by their commentaries and glossed halakhic compilations and scholarly needs promoted the adoption of the new ruling instrument by Franco-German Hebrew scribes.

Hence Hebrew medieval booklore may be classified into five main geocultural entities: Ashkenazic, Italian, Byzantine, Sephardic and Oriental (figure 18). However, conspicuous local peculiarities of script, and in some cases scribal practices, fully justify the singling out of two Oriental sub-entities, that of Iran and its neighbours, such as Uzbekistan, which we term Persian type, and that of South Arabia, designated as Yemenite type.

The various types of the medieval Hebrew book script have three fundamental operational modes – square, semi-cursive and cursive. The three modes were simultaneously employed in most of the geocultural entities and types of script, but only in the Sephardic territories had a fully current cursive developed by the twelfth century. In other types of script, the Ashkenazic and the Italian, for instance, current cursive writing emerged only in the sixteenth century, while the Oriental script never really acquired such a mode, and its later development was the result of the diffusion of the Sephardic scripts around the Mediterranean basin following the expulsion of the Jews from Spain and Portugal at the end of the fifteenth century. Following the settle-ment of expelled Spanish Jews in Italy, and particularly in Greece, the Balkans, Turkey, Syria, Palestine and Egypt, and their intellectual domination, the medieval typology of the Hebrew script was shaken and reshaped under the strong impact of the Sephardic scripts on the local ones. Later migrations of many *conversos* from Spain and particularly Portugal, to the Netherlands, Hamburg, and southern France introduced the Sephardic writings even into Ashkenaz. It seems that gradually a new type of script evolved all over the Ottoman Empire, a mixture of the Sephardic, the Oriental and Byzantine types that may be called an Ottoman type of Hebrew script.

The differences between the modes of each type basically involve the number of strokes required in producing the shape of a letter. The letters of the square scripts are formed by many more strokes than those of the semi-cursive ones; those of the cursive scripts are executed by an even smaller number of strokes, while the number of strokes is reduced to one for most letters in the current cursive shapes. However, cursiveness was not always achieved by reducing the number of strokes, but accomplished by quicker writing which combined several strokes without lifting the reed or quill pen. In the cursive grade of writing, noticeably in the Sephardic type, part of one letter or the entire letter would be combined with the following letter, or even several letters, all executed without lifting the pen (figure 19).

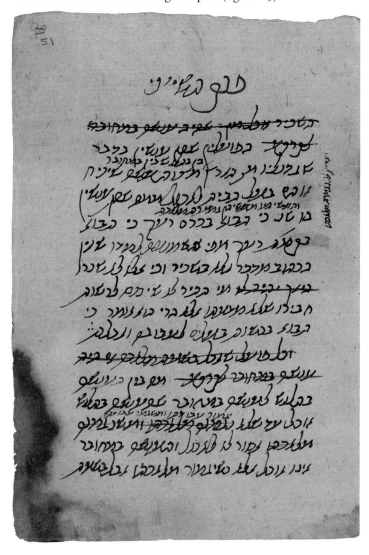

Figure 19
Maimonides' autograph draft of his legal code, *Mishneh Torah*, in cursive Sephardic script (Egypt, *c*. 1180). Oxford, Bodleian Library, MS. Heb. d. 32, fol. 51r.

In general, the square mode, which must have crystallized in the Orient as a calligraphic script for formal copies of the masoretic version of the Bible before the tenth century, and whose inception can be noticed already in the late formal script of the Dead Sea Scrolls and the Byzantine Hebrew papyri, was employed in all regions in the production of elegant or deluxe copies, particularly of biblical, liturgical and Talmudic texts, or for singling out glossed texts incorporated into commentaries. The cursive mode, which first evolved as an informal script used for private records, drafts and letters, was partly adopted as a book script, mainly in owner-produced copies and compilations.

The threefold execution of Hebrew medieval book script in fact multiplies the number of its types and subtypes, as the shapes of most of the letters in each mode of a type are entirely different from each other. Consequently, the number of distinctive shapes of writing increases to fifteen species, disregarding considerable transformations over the six centuries of extant Hebrew codices.

References

M. Beit-Arié, *Hebrew Codicology: Tentative Typology of Technical Practices Employed in Hebrew Dated Medieval Manuscripts* (Jerusalem, 1981).

— *Hebrew Manuscripts of East and West: Towards a Comparative Codicology* (The Panizzi Lectures) (London, 1993).

— *The Makings of the Medieval Hebrew Book: Studies in Palaeography and Codicology* (Jerusalem, 1993).

CHAPTER 3

Fables from East to West

César Merchán-Hamann

The narrative tradition of the Indian fable is a prime example of the encounter of cultures. The *Pañcatantra*, or *Fables of Bidpai*, was first translated into Pahlavi (Middle Persian), and thence into Syriac and Arabic, under the title of *Kalila and Dimna*. In Arabic literature the genre took root and became thoroughly assimilated, and from there it went on to make its mark on medieval Hebrew and Spanish literature, and through these, as well as through translations from the Arabic into Latin, it passed into every European language. Two other major works were translated into Syriac and Arabic, and then in turn into Hebrew and Old Spanish, Latin and most of the European languages: the *Book of Sindibad* and the *Barlaam and Josaphat*.[1] The role of the Jews as translators as well as of the Hebrew translations themselves was crucial to the development of this process.[2] Part of the explanation for the immense popularity of these works in the West seems to lie in the use that was made of the fables they contained as exempla in sermons.[3] The importance of the role of these three works lies not simply in the dissemination of the fables they contained, but also in their very structure: the technique of the frame-story in which the tales are embedded and that gives the narrative a structure and a purpose. This technique was adopted widely in Western Europe, and thus our collections constitute one of the most important sources for medieval Western narrative. Here, we shall concentrate on how the *Kalila and Dimna* crossed borders all the way from India to Iceland in the West and on one of the manifestations of creative appropriation which characterize the journey of this and similar works to the West, together with the vital role played by Hebrew translations and translators in the process.

The work is of Indian origin – the fables were collected and the frame story written around 300 CE, by a Brahmin scholar called Vishnu-

هذا المثل للأسد وأصحابه لأني أعرفهم إذا اجتمعوا على ملاكي
صفة الغراب والذئب وابن اوى وقد وثبوا على الجمل من يا

ولو كان ذلك مثل الحالة انهم سيظفرون بحاجتهم منه وقد فيل
ان السلطان من اشباه النسور يحولها الجيف لا الجيف حولها النسور كما

Figure 20 *far left*
Ibn al-Muqaffaʻs *Kalila wa-Dimna*, an Arabic adaptation of the Indian fable collection *Pañcatantra* (1354). Oxford, Bodleian Library, MS. Poc. 400, fol. 60r.

Figure 21 *left*
Kalila wa-Dimna: Jacob ben Eleazar's Hebrew translation from the Arabic, with a drawing of a jackal, one of the main characters of the fable collection (Ashkenaz, fifteenth century). Oxford, Bodleian Library, MS. Opp. Add. 4° 101, fol. 44v.

sharman, whose existence is uncertain. Its purpose was didactic, inculcating a pragmatic approach to politics which did not always conform to strict ethical norms. Beyond narrow instructive aims, however, the stories portray life in all its complexity and ambiguity – this contributed to the perennial appeal of the work.[4] In India it retained the original title, *Pañcatantra*.[5] From Sanskrit it was translated into Pahlavi around 550 CE. A Persian Muslim, Ibn al-Muqaffaʻ, rendered the work into Arabic in the eighth century (figure 20). His prose became a model for a forthright, expressive style, ideal for the diffusion of fictional works. The immense popularity of the collection contributed partly to the legitimization of fiction within Arabic literature, and led to its spread throughout the then Muslim world, which included the Iberian peninsula. The Spanish translation was made for King Alfonso the Wise in 1251, when still a prince (or possibly in 1261).[6] Ángeles Navarro Peiró has drawn attention to the role of Jews as translators in Christian Spain, noting the importance of Jacob ben Eleazar of Toledo's translation, of which more follows.[7] Another medieval version worthy of note is the Byzantine Greek rendering, since the Balkans constituted another gate for the entrance of Eastern fable collections into Europe.

There are two Hebrew translations: the first one, by Rabbi Joel, was executed before 1278 and possibly as early as the end of the twelfth century – unfortunately the extant manuscript is incomplete; the other version, by Jacob ben Eleazar of Toledo, author of an original collection of fables – the *Sefer ha-meshalim*, is less faithful to the original, but his translation is significant for its skilful incorporation of the rhymed prose technique from Arabic literature[8] (figure 21). The work was transmitted to other parts of Western Europe when it was rendered into Latin in two different versions. Johannes of Capua's *Directorium humanae vitae* (c. 1263–78) was translated from the first Hebrew version and was the best known of the Latin renderings[9] (figure 22). The second version, the *Liber Kalilae et Dimnae* (finished in 1313) by Raimundus de Biterris, was composite: the first half was translated from the Spanish while the second half was taken from Capua's *Directorium*.[10] This early transmission to the West would thus have been impossible without the Hebrew versions, for without them no translation into Latin would have been achieved.

The story of the transmission of the *Book of Sindibad* is more complex. Its origins are the subject of debate,[11] since the source of the work has not survived, and the extant versions are grouped in two branches: the Eastern branch, usually referred to as the *Book of Sindibad*, with eight surviving versions (Syriac, Greek, Old Spanish, Arabic, Hebrew and three in Persian), and the Western branch. The *Book of Sindibad* was translated into Spanish for Alfonso's brother, the Infante Don Fadrique, in 1253, and into Hebrew some time before 1295; this is the only version of the Eastern branch of the collection to have reached Western Europe. The Western branch, on the other hand, derived from two Latin translations, one by Johannes de Alta Silva, as the *Dolopathos sive de rege et septem sapientibus* (end of the twelfth or beginning of the thirteenth century) and one by an unknown translator, as the *Liber de septem sapientibus*, dating from around 1135; from the latter derive all the Western European versions, known as the *Seven Sages of Rome*.[12]

The *Barlaam and Josaphat*, originally one of the Indian legends of Buddha's life story, achieved extraordinary popularity in the Christian world, where it was christianized to such a point that its protagonists were venerated as saints. It was translated into Spanish, from a Latin intermediary text, either in the late thirteenth or in the fourteenth century, and into Hebrew by Abraham Ibn Hasdai of Barcelona in the first half of the thirteenth century, under the title *Ben ha-melekh ve-ha-nazir*. This last work was no mere translation, but rather a creative reworking and adaptation of the original in rhymed prose.[13] Through the Greek or Latin translations it reached most of Western Europe.[14]

Very influential, too, was the *Disciplina clericalis*, a collection of exempla translated into Latin by the Aragonese Jewish convert Moshe Sefaradi (better known as Petrus Alphonsi) early in the twelfth century, and which already contains several of the stories later to be found in the translations of the *Kalila and Dimna* and the *Book of Sindibad*, showing that many of the tales were already known in the Mediterranean world.[15] It became immensely popular in Europe, as the numerous extant manuscripts attest.[16]

The four works mentioned above were translated into nearly every European language, and it is enough to list a few of the works which betray their influence, together with their approximate dates of composition, to give an idea of their importance to the development of Western narrative: *Il Novellino* (1290), *El Conde Lucanor* (1320), *El Libro de Buen Amor* (1340), *Gesta Romanorum* (1340) the *Decameron* (1350), *The Canterbury Tales* (1390), and the *Confessio amantis* (1390). These works in turn deeply affected all subsequent European narrative. As mentioned above, the nature of the influence was twofold: not only were many of the individual stories borrowed, but the technique of the frame-story which contains them was adopted as well. The role of the Jews in this process has already been remarked upon, among many others by Moritz Steinschneider, as already intimated in the title of his work: *Die Juden als Dolmetscher* (the Jews as interpreters). Eli Yassif, who translates the term *Dolmetscher* as 'intermediaries' rather than 'interpreters', has remarked in a slightly different context that it was the Hebrew manuscripts more than the Jews themselves that played the role of intermediaries.[17]

In the ninth century, the process of acceptance of fiction was under way in Arabic literature, mainly as a result of the exposure to Persian literary models, including among many others the narrative works already mentioned. This process was far from unproblematic, but one of the few genres that escaped the initial opprobrium which attached to fiction in the Muslim Arabic literary world was that of the collections of fables, and this contributed to the popularity of the *Kalila and Dimna* and, to a lesser extent, maybe because of the more significant presence of human characters, to the diffusion of the *Book of Sindibad* and the tale of *Barlaam and Josaphat*.[18]

Fiction became an increasingly respected genre of Arabic literature. Particularly popular was the new genre of the *maqāma* (pl. *maqāmāt*), a collection of tales in rhymed prose, interspersed with short poems, a common narrator and, only revealed at the very end, a single protagonist, who appears in disguise in each tale. One of the finest collections of *maqāmāt* was written by al-Harīrī in Baghdad (d. 1122). The collection and with it the genre were eventually accepted, and gained canonical status, but at a cost, for the genre tended to avoid fiction and laid emphasis on form and moralizing to the detriment of the narrative.[19]

The collections of *maqāmāt* soon spread from one end of the Mediterranean to the other, and in Spain they were soon translated into Hebrew, with Judah ben Solomon al-Harizi (1170–1235) translating the

Figure 22
Directorium humanae vitae: Johannes of Capua's Latin translation from the Hebrew version of *Kalila wa-Dimna*. Printed in Strasbourg by Johann Prüss (*c.*1489). Oxford, Bodleian Library, Douce 193, fol. [23r].

collection of al-Harīrī, to which he gave the title *Mahberot Itiel*, no later than 1218.[20] The translation itself is generally considered a masterpiece. Creative appropriation rather than simple borrowing had to be effected in order to render the word-play and allusiveness of the original into the Hebrew language. The specific social and cultural conditions in which these works came to be written have to be kept in mind. In the Middle Ages, the main model for Hebrew prose of the sort we are dealing with was Biblical Hebrew, and biblical phrases tended to be used not simply for their suitability to express a given idea, but could also call to the mind of the audience the full gamut of meanings associated with it in its specific scriptural context. Biblical phrases had the additional role of matching the ending of the phrase with the adjacent one so as to conform to the requirements of the rhymed prose scheme. It would seem that this kind of literary production was written for a biblically literate audience. The dependence on a sophisticated audience capable of grasping the subtleties implicit in the text suggests those present would have been willing to appreciate the laborious process of translation. No doubt the author would have received recognition for his work that could take the form of a financial reward.[21]

In this context a good example would be the above-mentioned two versions of the *Kalila and Dimna* – the earlier of the two, by Rabbi Joel, is closer to the literal meaning of the Arabic original; the latter one, however, by Jacob ben Eleazar of Toledo (author of the collection of *maqāmāt* in Hebrew, *Sefer ha-meshalim*), although of necessity not as faithful to the original due to the use of rhymed prose, is according to Girón-Negrón 'a model of Hebrew translation and *recomposition*' (my emphasis).[22] In a short space, the Jewish audience in Castile, or at least a part of it, had made the production of such a sophisticated literary work possible. Furthermore, although Jewish tradition furnished the author with the resources, the genre itself did not belong to the religious sphere, whilst the content of the texts which used the genre – although of an ostensibly moral and didactic character – was not overtly Jewish. This was indeed an example of the successful transposition of a genre in a manner that re-created the form using dissimilar materials displaying parallel but not necessarily identical functions.

Judah ben Solomon al-Harizi, translator of the collection of *maqāmāt* of al-Harīrī, went on to compose his own collection of *maqāmāt* some time after 1220, the *Sefer Tahkemoni*, in which he demonstrated his mastery of the genre. But it is not only as a literary master that he is to be reckoned with, but also as one of the first authors to write this type of work in Hebrew rather than in Arabic. By 1281, a later figure of the Hispanic Jewish literary community, Isaac ben Solomon Ibn Sahula (b.

1244) would compose in Hebrew the *Meshal ha-qadmoni*, a collection of *maqāmāt* with the express purpose of supplanting works such as the *Kalila and Dimna*, producing instead original Hebrew creations (figure 23).[23]

The *Meshal ha-qadmoni* is much more than a narrative work, combining as it does comparatively large doses of philosophical, scientific and linguistic knowledge. The narrative parts include allusions to contemporary political events, carefully evaluated by Raphael Loewe, which show an intimate involvement with the Christian society in which the author resided.[24] This leads to an interesting fact that must be noted here – it was only when the Christian kingdoms had achieved the Reconquista of most of the Iberian peninsula from the Muslims that the development of Hebrew narrative prose genres in Spain really achieved a steady momentum. This would seem to imply a change in social conditions generating needs beyond the simple production of material destined to entertain, edify and educate; what seems to be at issue here is a programme aimed at developing the linguistic range of

Figure 23

Meshal ha-qadmoni (The Fable of the Ancient) by Isaac ben Solomon Ibn Sahula (Ashkenaz, 1450). Oxford, Bodleian Library, MS. Opp. 154, fols 42v–43r.

the Hebrew language; Raphael Loewe surmises that this was possibly
with a view to its adoption as a spoken language, although this was not
actually stated in so many words by the author. Whatever the validity
of this claim, it is undeniable that the work does aim to transmit a
considerable amount of learning in what Ibn Sahula considered to be
the most essential branches of knowledge.[25]

That the audience for the work must have enjoyed a high level of
prosperity is attested to by the fact that the author had the work illustrated, and he probably even provided the illustrations himself. If this
was not the case, he must have had to hire a professional artist, thus
adding considerably to the already high costs of production. Although
the original manuscript has not survived and thus we have no chance
of seeing the original illustrations, the tradition of adding pictures to
the *Meshal ha-qadmoni* itself – as well as to fable collections in general
– endured into the printed editions of the work (figure 24).

Ultimately, the *maqāma* genre did not thrive in Hebrew literature.
The social conditions required for its production were of a very high
level. As mentioned above, the intricacy of allusion not only restricted
its audience but, even more importantly, diverted its attention from the
narrative. This does not mean that the genre did not enjoy continued
success, as attested to by multiple printings of the main collections of

maqāmāt, but rather that after the end of the fourteenth century the production of new collections gradually ebbed and, although it never completely ceased, it did not enjoy the same measure of success ever again. It went well beyond the confines of the Iberian peninsula, and in Italy the genre received its supreme exponent when Immanuel of Rome (1261–after 1328) composed his *Mahbarot*. In fact, none of the extant manuscripts of the *Meshal ha-qadmoni* can be traced to the Iberian peninsula – the majority of them are of Italian origin.

The texts assembled are witnesses to a journey – the travellers, manuscripts containing tales and a set of literary techniques that travelled with them. In the course of this journey the travellers changed and became acclimatized in each of the lands and cultures where they stopped. At the end of the journey the voyagers had changed significantly, but not to the point that they cannot be recognized. This remarkable journey was undertaken to a great extent by Hebrew texts, and there is no better testimony to the success of the travellers than the multiplicity and the richness of the traditions that they engendered.

NOTES

1. Some of the languages into which these works were translated include: Pahlavi (Middle Persian), Syriac, Arabic, Old Ethiopic, Byzantine Greek, Old Spanish, Old Church Slavonic, Latin, Old French, Middle English, Scots, Old Norse, Middle High German, Old Georgian, Armenian, Ottoman Turkish, Persian, Portuguese, Catalan, Occitan, Italian, Czech, Polish, Romanian, Russian, Modern Icelandic, Danish, Swedish, Hungarian.
2. See M. Steinschneider, *Die hebräischen Übersetzungen des Mittelalters und die Juden als Dolmetscher* (Berlin, 1893) for an overview of this role.

3. A.D. Deyermond, *Historia de la Literatura Española: La Edad Media* (Madrid, 1973), 114, 176–81.

4. Visnuśarman, *The Five Discourses on Worldly Wisdom* (New York, 2006), 18–19.

5. For a succint review of the origins of the work and its place within the Indian tradition, see P. Olivelle's introduction to his translation in the Clay Sanskrit Library bilingual edition of *Five Discourses*, ibid., 17–48.

6. On the problems surrounding its dating, see J.M. Cacho Blecua and M. J. Lacarra, eds, *Calila e Dimna* (Madrid, 1985), 14–19.

7. A. Navarro Peiró, 'La versión hebrea de Calila y Dimna de Ya'aqob ben El'azar', in J. Targarona Borrás and Á. Sáenz-Badillos, eds., *Jewish Studies at the Turn of the Twentieth Century*, Vol. 1: *Biblical, Rabbinical, and Medieval Studies* (Leiden, 1999), 468–75, *passim*.

8. A. Navarro Peiró, *Narrativa hispanohebrea: siglos XII–XV* (Córdoba, 1988), 23–6.

9. Johannes de Capua, *Directorium Humanae Vitae, alias Parabolae Antiquorum Sapientum* (Pisa, 1884).

10. For further details, as well as a clarification of Raimundus's supposed plagiarism of Johannes de Capua, see B. Taylor, 'Raimundus de Biterris's *Liber Kalile et Dimne*: Notes on the Western Reception of an Eastern *Exemplum*-Book', in D. Hook and B. Taylor, eds, *Cultures in Contact in Medieval Spain* (London, 1990), 183–203 at 186–90.

11. Arguments have been put forward for Sanskrit, Persian or Hebrew origins.

12. M.J. Lacarra, ed., *Sendebar* (Madrid, 1989), 18–19. Morris Epstein, ed. and trans., *Tales of Sendebar* (Philadelphia, 1967), 12–13, 333–9.

13. See Abraham ben Hisdai, *The Prince and the Monk* (in Hebrew) (Tel Aviv, 1950).

14. Deyermond, *Historia*, 181; Navarro Peiró, *Narrativa*, 29–30.

15. See the introduction by M.J. Lacarra to Pedro Alfonso, *Disciplina clericalis* (Zaragoza, 1980).

16. As Schwarzbaum noted, there is even a Hebrew translation of the first two exempla, the *Sefer Hanokh*: Haim Schwarzbaum, 'International Folklore Motifs in Petrus Alfonsi's *Disciplina Clericalis*', in *Jewish Folklore between East and West* (Beer-Sheva, 1961–63), 258–9.

17. Eli Yassif, *The Hebrew Collection of Tales in the Middle Ages* (in Hebrew) (Tel Aviv, 2004), 24–5.

18. See R. Drory, 'Legitimizing Fiction in Classical Arabic', in *Models and Contacts: Arabic Literature and Its Impact on Medieval Jewish Culture* (Leiden, 2000), 37–47, for a concise view of the process.

19. The genre and its acceptance in Arabic literature are capably dealt with by Drory, *Models and Contacts*, 11–36, 111–21.

20. *Mahberet* (pl. *mahbarot*) was the Hebrew translation of the term *maqāma*.

21. See the introduction and commentaries to the individual sections in the English anthology of medieval Hebrew narrative by D. Stern and M. Mirsky, *Rabbinic Fantasies: Imaginative Narratives from Classical Hebrew Literature* (New Haven, 1998). For a treatment of the collections of tales in medieval Hebrew literature, see Yassif, *The Hebrew Collection of Tales*. For a precis of the present state of the scholarship on medieval Hebrew literature, see T. Rosen and E. Yassif, 'The Study of Hebrew Literature in the Middle Ages: Major Trends and Goals', in Martin Goodman, ed., *The Oxford Handbook of Jewish Studies* (Oxford, 2002), 241–94.

22. L.M. Girón-Negrón, 'How the Go-Between Cut Her Nose: Two Ibero-Medieval Translations of a Kalilah wa-Dimnah Story', in C. Robinson and L. Rouhi, eds, *Under the Influence: Questioning the Comparative in Medieval Castile* (Leiden, 2004), 231–59 at 255.

23. For more information on the composition and structure of the *Meshal ha-qadmoni*, see the comprehensive introduction by R. Loewe to his translation of the work, in itself a work of poetic re-creation worthy of the original, and on which I have drawn for most of my facts: Isaac ben Solomon Ibn Sahula, *Meshal Haqadmoni: Fables from the Distant Past*, Vol. 1 (Oxford, 2004), xv–cxxxi.

24. Ibn Sahula, *Meshal*, lxxxvi–c.

25. R. Loewe has examined the contents of the philosophical, linguistic and scientific interpolations in the narrative material and commented on the large measure of correspondence between them and the contemporary educational curriculum as well as with the programme of educational reform undertaken by Alfonso X the Learned of Castile, Ibn Sahula's contemporary. *Meshal*, lix–lxix.

CHAPTER 4

Early Ashkenazic Prayer Books and Their Christian Illuminators

Eva Frojmovic

Sabbath, fasts and festivals marked sacred time, creating an invisible enclosure around the Jewish community. Not that Jews lived separate lives from Christians; rather, because their lives were so intricately intertwined, the minority needed to assert its religious identity by structuring time and space.[1] What made Jewish time visible and concrete were synagogues and prayer books. Books allow us to re-create the visual world of the medieval Jewish community. Their decoration can tell us much about how Jewish communities imagined themselves and how they related to their non-Jewish surroundings. This contribution is devoted to prayer books from German- and Yiddish-speaking Ashkenaz (Germany, Austria, Bohemia, Poland).

The three great books discussed here are *mahzorim*; that is, festival prayer books. They were not used on ordinary weekdays or normal Sabbath days, but only on festivals, fast days, and the four special Sabbath days leading up to Passover. Whereas the prayer book used for weekdays and the Sabbath is called a *siddur* (derived from the Hebrew word for 'order' – of service), the book used on festivals is the *mahzor* (literally, 'cycle'). And whereas modern prayer books are produced for the ordinary worshippers, the large-format *mahzorim* of thirteenth-century German lands were copied for the prayer leader, whether a professional cantor (*hazzan*), a rabbi or a lay member of the community. The prayer leader (and his congregation, most of whom could not afford books) knew the fixed prayers by heart, or could use a *siddur* to recite them. Very few of the actual prayers are written out in the Ashkenazic *mahzorim*; usually, only the initial words are included for cross-reference.[2] Instead, the *mahzorim* are filled almost entirely with the hymns (*piyyutim*) composed by many generations of poets between late antiquity and high medieval Europe. These *piyyutim* are long, intricate and linguistically complex. Thousands of them have survived to this day. Different communities compiled collections that were specific to them and embodied their cherished local tradition. A medieval Ashkenazic *mahzor* is thus a collection of festival hymns encapsulating the liturgical identity of its community.[3]

Oxford's Hebraica collections are uniquely rich in early prayer books from Ashkenaz. Corpus Christi College preserves the oldest *siddur* from Christian Europe, compiled in England before 1202 (CCC MS. 133). The Bodleian Library owns the oldest dated *mahzor* (MSS. Mich. 617 and 627, 1257/8), which is also illuminated. And so, with the help of a number of other thirteenth- and fourteenth-century illuminated *mahzorim*, we are in the exceptional position of being able to reconstruct the early development of the Ashkenazic *mahzor*.

The earliest prayer books north of the Alps were small in format, indicating that they were meant for individual users. Whereas the late-twelfth-century English *siddur* at Corpus Christi College is a very plain book, written mostly in single columns and without decoration, the same cannot be said of the early French prayer books in the Bodleian Library. Despite their small formats (for example, two incomplete volumes of an early-thirteenth-century French *mahzor*, MSS. Opp. 670 and 669, measure 17.5 × 11.5 cm), they have been copied with considerable attention to design: pages are ruled to allow for decorative text layouts (hourglass shapes were especially popular) and initial words are decorated with delicate pen-drawn and washed vegetal and animal patterns.

Initially, the same modest format was used in German Ashkenaz: the early thirteenth-century German *mahzor* MS. Opp. 671 measures 18.4 × 14.2 cm. Around the middle of the thirteenth century, however, the format changed significantly. The two-volume Michael Mahzor (MSS. Mich. 617, 627) dated 1257/8, is a heavy, large-format book (40 × 30 cm); the later thirteenth-century Laud Mahzor (MS. Laud Or. 321) is even larger (45 × 32.5–34 cm); the early-fourteenth-century Tripartite Mahzor (MS. Mich. 619), though smaller at 35.5 × 27.5 cm, is still significantly larger than its predecessors from the first half of the thirteenth century. This grand format can be found in most illuminated *mahzorim* from thirteenth- and fourteenth-century German lands.[4] They were not held in the hand, but had to rest on a lectern.

These books did more than transmit a text. They carried 'added value' and cultural capital by being set out on extra-large sheets of fine and expensive parchment, with generous margins. They were written out in large letters and in neat columns (thus consuming more expensive parchment). And, just as important, they were decorated with ambitious pen drawings or coloured and gilded illuminations.

Many of the scribes were consummate draftsmen. Their pen-drawn decorations were just as sophisticated as the coloured illuminations of professional painters that are my focus here.

Who were these large-format hymn books intended for? And who paid for them to be copied on large quantities of expensive parchment and to be illuminated? The answer I propose is that they were privately commissioned by wealthy Jewish householders wishing to emulate aristocratic patronage, and that they were destined to be used in a communal context, to be publicly visible.

Jewish Patrons in a Christian World

As Professor Malachi Beit-Arié has pointed out, there was a fundamental difference between the way in which Latin and Hebrew books were produced.[5] Within the wider Christian society, powerful institutions, especially courts, cathedrals and monasteries, were able to support scriptoria (writing workshops); by contrast, Jewish book production was entirely a private, not an institutional, matter. Throughout most of the medieval period, the majority of Hebrew manuscripts were user-produced; that is to say, texts were copied out by scholars or students for their own use. But during the period between *c.* 1250 and the Black Death epidemic of 1347/8, we find another pattern of production and use: many of the large and elaborately decorated prayer books were apparently used in public, by the prayer leader, during the communal performance of the liturgy. We can draw this conclusion thanks to the evidence of the famous Worms Mahzor of 1272, whose colophon alludes to the patron's performance of the liturgy.[6] Likewise, the Leipzig Mahzor's opening miniature of a cantor and two assistants performing from his lectern is hardly casual.[7] The prayer leader was not necessarily a professional cantor – wealthy laymen vied with each other for the honour of leading prayers on festive occasions. These were the very men who commissioned large and splendidly decorated prayer books as status symbols, who owned them but also made them available to the community, and who sometimes bequeathed them to their community at their death. They mediated between the private space of book production and ownership and the communal arena of the synagogue.

Jewish patronage was predicated on private ownership, but the status of the Jewish patron – not a hereditary status as that of the Christian nobility was – was conferred and confirmed by the community. Status in the community was acquired either through rabbinic scholarship or through the charitable use of wealth. One form of such use of wealth was the commissioning of books, which, as in Christian culture, also served as status symbols. Indeed, the social

Figure 25 *below*
The Michael Mahzor, the
earliest dated *mahzor*
(Germany, 1257/8). Oxford,
Bodleian Library, MS.
Mich. 617, fol. 21r.

Figure 26 *right*
Michael Mahzor:
The Zodiac cycle
accompanying the prayer
for rain for Passover:
Aries, Taurus and
Gemini (with bird
heads, according to early
Ashkenazic tradition).
Oxford, Bodleian Library,
MS. Mich. 617, fol. 49v.

Figure 27 *far right*
Michael Mahzor:
Opening hymn for the
"Sabbath of the Shekel".
The illumination (upside
down) reveals the hand
of a Christian illustrator.
Oxford, Bodleian Library,
MS. Mich. 617, fol. 4v.

role of books in the Jewish community was arguably greater than in the surrounding Christian society. Jewish patrons sought to enhance their status by employing the most sought-after professional scribes, by commissioning larger and larger volumes, and by resorting to the most professional illuminators – often Christian artists. In fact, it is likely that all three of the great Bodleian *mahzorim* – the Michael, Laud and Tripartite Mahzorim – were illuminated by Christian painters in collaboration with and under the supervision of Jewish scribes.

The Bodleian's Hebrew Festival Prayer Books and the Involvement of Christian Artists

The Michael Mahzor (MS. Mich. 617/627) is the earliest dated *mahzor* known. Its two volumes (for winter and summer) were completed between September 1257 and September 1258 by the scribe Judah bar Samuel 'Zaltman', as he recorded in monumental lettering on the last folio of the second volume.[8] The Michael Mahzor is not only the earliest dated *mahzor*, but also the earliest *mahzor* with painted illuminations. Its layout presupposes a high level of integration between scribe and painter: monumental-sized initial words are enveloped in panels enclosing human and animal figures. Only a few of these relate to the text: the hanging of Haman and his ten sons (MS. Mich. 617, fol. 16, accompanying a hymn for Purim); the red heifer for the Sabbath on which the Torah portion of the red heifer is read (MS. Mich. 617, fol. 21r (figure 25), though, curiously, the artist has included three cows instead of one); the sun, moon, and star for the Sabbath inaugurating the spring month of Nissan (MS. Mich. 617, fol. 26); and the Zodiac cycle accompanying the prayer for rain for Passover (MS. Mich. 617, fols 49v–51v, figure 26). Apart from this cycle, which spans only one month, the rest of the *mahzor* is illuminated with subjects that can hardly be said to illustrate the text: riders, hunters and fighters; animals both tame and wild; and dragons playing, chasing and fighting among stylized foliage. These are no religious images, either Jewish or Christian. Rather, they are functional, in creating clear divisions within the prayer book and thus enabling the users to find their way round the text.

What makes the images culturally specific is their reluctance to show the human face: faces are either covered by helmets (as on fol. 4v, figure

27) or replaced by animal heads.[9] This concealment of the human face harks back to a mode of representation that had been pioneered in South Germany a generation earlier. In the 1230s, the illuminators of the South German so-called Ambrosian Bible[10] had given some of the biblical and rabbinic protagonists animal faces in order to satisfy Jewish sensibilities regarding rabbinic strictures against idolatrous images. By making their creations into hybrid creatures, the painters in effect 'cancelled' the very 'idolatrous images' they were creating. The large *mahzorim* of the second half of the century build on those early experiments with figuration.

At the very beginning of the first volume, the reader may be disconcerted to find that the illuminated panel at the opening hymn for the 'Sabbath of the Shekel' lies upside down in relation to the text (figure 27). There is only one explanation: not only could the painter not read the text, but he was unfamiliar with the appearance of the Hebrew alphabet. The writing proceeds from the 'back' of the book to the 'front', with the letters progressing on their lines from right to left (rather than left to right) and suspended from the ruled line (rather than poised on it); the painter sought to right the unnatural order – as he saw it – by standing the page upside down before painting it. Turned upside down, the page looked rather like a Latin page in format. The error occurs only

Figure 28 *below*
Michael Mahzor, 'Ayelet Ahavim', prayer for the second day of Shavuot. Oxford, Bodleian Library, MS. Mich. 617, fol. 99r.

מִתְנַשֵּׂא לְכֹל לְרֹאשׁ ׀ בְּחַרְבָּאוּ
כְּאוּם דָּלֶת רֹאשׁ ׀ כְּבְבֹורַח כְּתַאֲנַךְ
בָּרֹאשׁ ׀ בְּיָטָה וְאַתָּה דָּרוֹשׁ ׀ מִכָּל
אוּם לְפָרוֹשׁ ׀ רְּנַשֵּׂא עַל כֹּל לְרֹאשׁ ׀
יַעֲלֶה תָּשִׁית לְמִנְּוֹד רֹאשׁ ׀ וְהָיוּ
תָרִים רֹאשׁ ׀ בְּכִסֵּא כָבֹוד מֵרֹאשׁ ׀

once in the entire *mahzor*. It seems that Judah bar Samuel 'Zaltman' then took control and supervised the illuminator more closely. So here we find the Jewish scribe in a supervisory position in relation to the Christian illuminator. In any case, the scribe and the painter were in contact, possibly passing individual quires back and forth as they were being written. Certainly, the scribe had 'the last word': he vocalized some of the initial words, now framed in the painted panels, after the illuminations' completion (visible for example in MS. Mich. 617, fol. 99r (figure 28), 'Ayelet Ahavim' for the second day of Shavuot (Pentecost); MS. Mich. 627, fol. 59, 'Barukh … ha-poteah lanu sha'arei rahamim' for Yom Kippur (Day of Atonement)).

This *mahzor* must have been an admired prototype for later copies, because numerous figures were traced with a heavy leadpoint. Curiously, only the animals, never the human hunters and fighters, were copied. It could be suggested that the copyists did not simply appropriate the images uncritically, but rather chose those that served their purpose.

The Laud Mahzor (MS. Laud Or. 321) is the largest of the three *mahzorim*, and is bound in a single volume. We do not know when it was completed, but it is datable on stylistic grounds to the period between 1270 and 1280. Several hands appear to have contributed to its decoration, all of which is of very fine quality. In this *mahzor* we encounter a much more carefully controlled iconographic programme. True, the large arched frontispiece on fol. 38v (figure 29) (in fact, it is the opening of the hymn for Sabbath Shekalim, which was also originally the opening folio of the *mahzor*) is distinguished by a gateway whose arch is decorated with a hare hunt – a neutral theme in this period, not related to the text. But most of the remaining

Figure 29
Laud Mahzor: Opening hymn for the 'Sabbath of the Shekel'. Jewish users have traced over the illustration so many times that it finally cracked. (Ashkenaz, 1270s). Oxford, Bodleian Library, MS. Laud Or. 321, fol. 38v.

Figure 30 *above*
Laud Mahzor.
top Giving of the Law.
bottom Baking of the
bread sacrificed on
Shavuot. Oxford, Bodleian
Library, MS. Laud Or. 321,
fol. 127v.

Figure 31 *right*
Tripartite Mahzor: Initial
word of the opening
prayer for the Day of
Atonement (*Kol nidrei*;
Ashkenaz, fourteenth
century). Oxford,
Bodleian Library, MS.
Mich. 619, fol. 100v.

illuminated pages can be directly related to the festival they accompany: Ahasuerus handing Esther his sceptre (fol. 48v) and the Hanging of Haman and his sons (fol. 51) for Purim; the red heifer facing the high priest with his hyssop sprig (fol. 53) for Shabbat Parah; the Zodiac signs illustrating the prayer for dew (fol. 89–91), the Egyptians pursuing the Israelites for Pesach (fol. 108), the giving of the Torah and the baking of the bread sacrificed on Shavuot (fol. 127v, figure 30), and the Binding of Isaac (fol. 184) for Rosh Hashanah, a Sukkah (fol. 312v) and a Jew with Lulav and Etrog (fol. 320) for Sukkot. All these are biblical themes appropriate to their respective festivals. Motifs from rabbinic sources are rare (angel with scales and scribe for Rosh Hashanah (fol. 165v)), but on fol. 97 a curious egg game accompanies one of the *piyyutim* for Passover, indicating long-forgotten customs.

The artists of the Laud Mahzor resorted to the – by then traditional – animal-headed disguise for most of the figures, and realized a very specific iconographic programme intimately tied to the content of the text. And yet it is certain that it was painted in a Christian workshop. For on several folios, brief instructions for the illuminator survive, scribbled in leadpoint.[11] And they are in Latin. There can be no doubt that they are part of a set of instructions, and not later additions, because in one or two places the illuminations have actually been painted over the rubbed-out but still faintly visible Latin words. Only a Christian workshop would plausibly require instructions in Latin.

The Tripartite ('three-part') Mahzor (MS. Mich. 619) contains the prayers for the New Year and the Day of Atonement only. Two other manuscripts, one in London (BL Add. 22413) and one in Budapest (Hungarian Academy of Sciences, Ms. 384), complete it to make up a full *mahzor* for the whole year – originally bound in two volumes. The work is signed but not dated by the scribe Hayyim, and it is only thanks to the style of the miniatures (which represent the pinnacle of the art of *mahzor* illumination) that we are able to date the Tripartite Mahzor to the early decades of the fourteenth century. Fol. 100v of the Oxford volume enables us to appreciate the superb quality of the paintings (figure 31). A full-page miniature has been assigned to the initial word of the opening prayer for the Day of Atonement, 'Kol' (*Kol nidrei*, 'All the vows…'). Yet the solemnity of the moment, when the great fast is begun in fear and trembling by a hushed community,

is countered by the levity of the nonsensical content of the paintings. At the top a hybrid creature grows a hooded human upper body, while a hissing dragon literally makes up its rear, and an old man's face grows on its stomach. Below, two more dragons, one sporting slender human hands, confront each other, hissing loudly. Where total silence should greet the cantor's utterance at the beginning of the great fast, the hissing of dragons is joined by the noise of the wind instrument played by the hooded human – not the solemn *shofar* but the popular *schalmei* or reed pipe (or possibly the *Hirtenschalmei* or shepherd's shawm, with a wider flared end), whose piercing sound could be heard at secular outdoor entertainments. The only miniature in this volume – the second half of the *mahzor* – that is related to the content of the book is the ram with his horn caught in a thicket on the opening miniature for the New Year (fol. 5v), alluding to the Binding of Isaac commemorated on the New Year (figure 32). The first part of the *mahzor* (now split between Budapest and London) contains far more iconographically relevant images than the second (to which the Oxford codex belongs), including the Revelation at Sinai (BL Add. 22413, fol. 3) and the gleaning Ruth (fol. 71) for Shavuot. In these scenes, only the women's faces were concealed behind animal 'masks'! Was the painting workshop Jewish? It was not. Sarit Shalev-Eyni traced its work to the Lake Constance region, and identified the Dominican convent of St Katharinental (on the south bank of the Rhine, west of Lake Constance – now Switzerland) in 1312 as one of the artist's patrons.[12]

What emerges clearly is that Jewish patrons and scribes did not live in a closed cultural enclave, but rather were part of a shared cultural sphere with Christians. That they accorded great importance to grand and beautiful books, and images, is evidenced by the rich holdings of the Bodleian Library, not least by the treasures discussed here.

NOTES

The author gratefully acknowledges the support of the Leverhulme Trust and the Arts and Humanities Research Council.

1. For the notions of Jewish time and space I am indebted to R. Bonfil, *Jewish Life in Renaissance Italy* (Berkeley, 1994).

2. The Nuremberg Mahzor (1331) is exceptional in this regard, in that it contains the full text of some of the basic prayers as well as the *piyyutim*. At 50 × 37 cm and 521 folios, it may be the largest of all *mahzorim*. The online facsimile is available on http://jnul.huji. ac.il/dl/mss-pr/mahzor-nuremberg.

מלך

מלך יזור גבורה לבֹ המקי
תפם יֹ נוזר קבוֹה
ויֹ היוֹ יזור יזור קמטה ישר שנכ כן
כיכשר ידבך היוזר אל ויתבֹ היזוֹ ותֹ
ומה הקמטה שהזוֹ יורך יופים שבֹ
טוב יורך יופים וגטר והזוֹ יחד וֹיֹ
ומשים שוהֹק ובכש על ישועתֹם טֹל
ישֹר ולֹך הזכיֹם כזם תרועה שהוֹן
יום ישועה והתחיל הפייט מלֹך יזוֹ
טֹזוֹ היֹליתהו תהיֹלה ויזחר כך התפוֹ
כֹרֹ כֹהֹ ובזֹל שוֹיך בגטוֹה יתבֹרֹל
שוֹיך כשתהגבר על היוזויות לך וֹרוֹע
עם בגטֹרה שהבֹקֹמטרה היֹה הישועֹה
יֹאשֹר טֹעֹויֹחֹ וֹך וֹרוֹעֹם בגטֹה וֹ
כשהֹק כוֹעֹם יכוֹל וֹבכֹט יתבו וֹשֹבֹ
כֹכשֹרֹורֹם ֹ בֹ בֹזֹי נקם וֹשֹהוֹק
וֹלבֹש בֹזֹי נקם ֹ והוֹו לֹמֹש שיֹנ טֹל
ישועה ֹ לֹצֹרֹיך ישיב יֹל חֹיֹקֹם ֹ פֹתֹ
כֹיֹרֹתֹם ֹ טֹוֹ ֹ וֹוֹר נטֹשֹטֹו שֹכֹבֹ טֹ
בֹלֹילֹה הֹעֹתֹוֹנֹה בֹזֹיֹך ֹ גֹ גֹמֹות
וֹכֹם ֹ הֹוֹא ֹ וֹבֹש לֹבֹש שֹלֹיֹטֹ ֹ ימֹים מֹיֹבֹש

א זזר גבורה

גזול שמך בגבורה
לבזרזע עם גבורה
גזרי נקם
לבש ביום נקם
לצריך ישיב אלהיקם
אות לבש
ימים מיבש
וגאות אפיקים מיבבש
בעשרה לבושים התאזר בקדושים
אٰ נארץ כסזר קדושים קדוש

מלֹך בֹ

מלֹך גֹ

מלֹך

3. See D. Stern, *'Joodse' kunst en de wording van het middeleeuwse joodse gebedenboek* ['Jewish' Art and the Making of the Medieval Jewish Prayer Book] (Amsterdam, 2007).

4. French *mahzorim* from the second half of the thirteenth century are extremely rare; the surviving evidence suggests that they never grew to the larger sizes of their German counterparts. The unique *mahzor* for Rosh Hashanah in a French private collection, written shortly before the expulsion of 1306, measures 295 × 220 mm. G. Sed-Rajna and S. Fellous, *Les Manuscrits hébreux enluminés des bibliothèques de France* (Leuven, 1994), 172–4.

5. M. Beit-Arié, *Hebrew Manuscripts in East and West: Towards a Comparative Codicology (The Panizzi Lectures)* (London, 1993), 81–3.

6. 'I, Simha ben Judah the scribe, have written this *mahzor* for my uncle R. Barukh b. Isaac in forty-four weeks, editing and arranging from beginning to end every prayer read by the *hazzan*, and have completed it, with the Almighty's help, on the 28th of Tevet in the 32nd year of the era [= 2 January 1272]. May the Lord privilege him to use it to thank, to praise, to chant, to laud the Creator of his soul and to bequeath it, as intended, as an act of piety, for his soul, for he means well; may his righteousness endure forever. And I, Simha the clerk, will give praise, thanks and glory to my Rock through my majestic labour which is beautiful and bright, which I have executed in faith and purity. May he grant me the privilege of seeing children and grandchildren busying themselves with the study of the Torah and may he save me from all anguish and trouble, Amen and Amen speedily.' Jerusalem, JNUL 4.781/1, fol. 217v. The Worms Mahzor's colophon is of exceptional importance. The Worms Mahzor was made for use not in Worms but probably in Würzburg. Whether or not its patron was a professional cantor, he certainly acted as one at least occasionally. The annotations left by generations of later Worms cantors provide strong evidence that the *mahzor* was suited for the cantorial lectern. During the patron's lifetime, the book was evidently housed at his home: a short Yiddish blessing is directed at the 'person who carries this *mahzor* to *shul* [synagogue].' Although the scribe states that the patron is his uncle, this family link does not mean that the Worms Mahzor belongs to the group of user-produced texts, since the scribe and his collaborators – one of whom was his father, named as a scribe from Nuremberg – clearly formed a highly professional workshop (even if a family business). An online facsimile is available at www.jnul.huji.ac.il/dl/mss/worms. Note that Simha ben Judah also copied, with the assistance of three different punctuators/masoretes, the Pentateuch MS. Laud Or. 324. M. Beit-Arié, *The Makings of the Medieval Hebrew Book* (Jerusalem: 1993), 155.

7. Leipzig Universitätsbibliothek Ms. V. 1102, fol. 27 (another very large-format *mahzor*: 49 × 36 cm, 404 folios in two volumes of 179 and 225 fols). See E. Katz and B. Narkiss, *Machsor Lipsiae, Leipzig Mahzor. 68 Faksimile-Tafeln der mittelalterlichen hebräischen illuminierten Handschrift aus dem Bestand der Universitäts-Bibliothek Leipzig* (Vaduz, 1964); *Machsor Lipsiae*. Virtuelle Bibliothek. Deutsches Historisches Museum, Universitätsbibliothek Leipzig, 2 CD-ROM.

8. MS. Mich. 627, fol. 174: 'I, Judah bar Samuel, called Zaltman, have written this *mahzor* [the patron's name has been erased by a later owner] and I completed it in the 18th year in the sixth millennium [September 1257–September 1258]. May the Lord [actually, 'The Place', a common euphemism for the divine name] guard him and grant him the merit of sons who occupy themselves with Torah and who keep the commandments. And may he and his seed use it for ever, Amen Amen Sela. [Be] strong and brave.'

9. These occur only in volume 1. MS. Mich. 617, fol. 49v (Passover, prayer for rain): the Zodiac sign of Gemini is represented by two people, one animal-headed and one bird-headed – not twins! Fol. 50v: Virgo is a bird-headed woman, crowned and dancing (?). Fol. 59 (Passover, Sabbath during the festival): a naked woman painted yellow, with a monkey face, riding backwards.

10. Milan, Biblioteca Ambrosiana B 30–32 inf., dated 1236–8.

11. Fol. 48v Ahasuerus and Esther inscribed 'Asvver[us]' and 'Hest[er]'; fol. 53 illegible; fol. 97 two men playing with eggs inscribed 'Lude[ntes] de ovis'; fol. 184 remains of inscription possibly spelling '[Isa]ac?' under figure of Isaac; fol. 321 inscription covered over by painting and illegible.

12. S. Shalev-Eyni, *Jews Among Christians: A Hebrew School of Illumination of the Lake Constance Region* (Turnhout: Brepols/Harvey Miller), forthcoming; 'Illuminierte hebräische Handschriften aus dem Bodensee–Raum', *Kunst und Architektur in der Schweiz* 51/3 (2000), 29–38. My thanks to Dr Shalev-Eyni for her advice.

CHAPTER 5

The Virgin and the Unicorn:
A Christian Symbol in a Hebrew Prayer Book

Piet van Boxel

Hebrew manuscript production in medieval Europe served many purposes. An essential part of the task of the scribe was to provide for the liturgical needs of the Jewish communities. Prayer books for daily use (*siddurim*) and for the festivals and High Holidays (*mahzorim*) were copied out for service in the synagogue or for private use. The extant *mahzorim* produced in the German lands are among the earliest examples of Hebrew book production in Europe.[1] Often beautifully illuminated, either in Christian workshops or by Jewish artists, they give us surprising and sometimes unpredictable insights into Jewish life and the relationship of Jewish individuals and communities with the wider society.

Though representing only one particular case, manuscript Canon. Or. 62 of the Bodleian Library may shed some light on the life of Jews in northern Italy in the second half of the fifteenth century. The manuscript belongs to the collection accumulated by Matteo Luigi Canonici, who was born in Venice in 1727 and joined the order of the Jesuits in 1743. Due to subsequent expulsions of the Jesuit Order – Jesuits were forced out of the kingdom of Naples in 1767 and the entire Society was expelled by order of Pope Clement XIV in 1773 – Canonici retired to Venice, where he devoted himself to the study of history, and collected among other things printed books and manuscripts. He had always hoped that the Jesuits would be readmitted, in which case he would have bequeathed his collections to the Society, but eventually he died at Treviso in 1805 and his collections passed to his brother Giuseppe. After his death the 3,550 manuscripts went to Giovanni Perissinotti; after many attempts to sell them, the Bodleian Library became the purchaser of the greater part in 1817.[2]

The manuscript under discussion consists of three parts: the Torah (Pentateuch) in Hebrew with the Targum (the Aramaic translation of the biblical text) and Rashi's commentary; the Haftarot, passages from the books of the Prophets which are read together with the weekly portion of the Torah; the Five Megillot, which are added to the service on the various festivals – Song of Songs on Passover, Ruth on Shavuot (Pentecost), Lamentations on the ninth of Av (commemoration of the destruction of the Temple), Ecclesiastes on Sukkot (Tabernacles) and Esther on Purim (commemoration of the rescue of the Jewish people of the ancient Persian Empire from Haman's plot to annihilate them). The combination Torah, Haftarot and Megillot places our manuscript in a widespread liturgical tradition. Similar combinations are found in fifteen other manuscripts in the Bodleian Library stretching from the early thirteenth to the sixteenth century and written in a Spanish (Sephardic), Italian (humanistic) or northern European (Ashkenazic) hand. Half of the manuscripts are illuminated or decorated in the form of a non-figurative or figurative Masorah (critical notes on the biblical text), coloured initials or rather primitive illuminations.[3] Our manuscript fits into this decorative tradition, but stands out by virtue of its unusual and superb illuminations.

Neither owner nor scribe nor illuminator is explicitly mentioned. Playfully revealed in the Masorah is the name Abraham, which is probably the name of the owner, a practice not uncommon in Hebrew manuscripts.[4] The manuscript is produced in various hands: the biblical text in Italian–Ashkenazic square script, the Aramaic translation in semi-square, Rashi's commentary on the Pentateuch in semi-cursive of Sephardic type and the commentaries on the five scrolls in Ashkenazic semi-cursive script.[5] This exceptional variety of hands does not give any indication of its provenance, but rather shows the mobility of Hebrew scribes and the diverse make-up of a Jewish community. The manuscript is dated 1471. From the luxurious way it is illuminated one may conclude that the owner was well-to-do and may have belonged to a thriving Jewish community. It is more than likely, as I will attempt to prove, that he was a Ferrarese Jew.

From 1240 to 1597 Ferrara was ruled by the d'Este family. Key players in the fifteenth century were the two bastard sons of Nicolò III, Leonello, who reigned from 1441 to 1450, and Borso, who ruled from 1450 to 1471. They were both celebrated patrons of the arts. Leonello had been educated by the humanist Guarino Veronese, called to Ferrara by his father, and during his reign the city became a centre of culture and art attracting painters such as Pisanello, Jacopo Bellini, Rogier van der Weyden and Andrea Mantegna. Borso's court remained the centre of artistic activity, of which the frescoes in the Palazzo Schifanoia are the most famous but not the only witness. It was also under this magnanimous patron that the art of manuscript

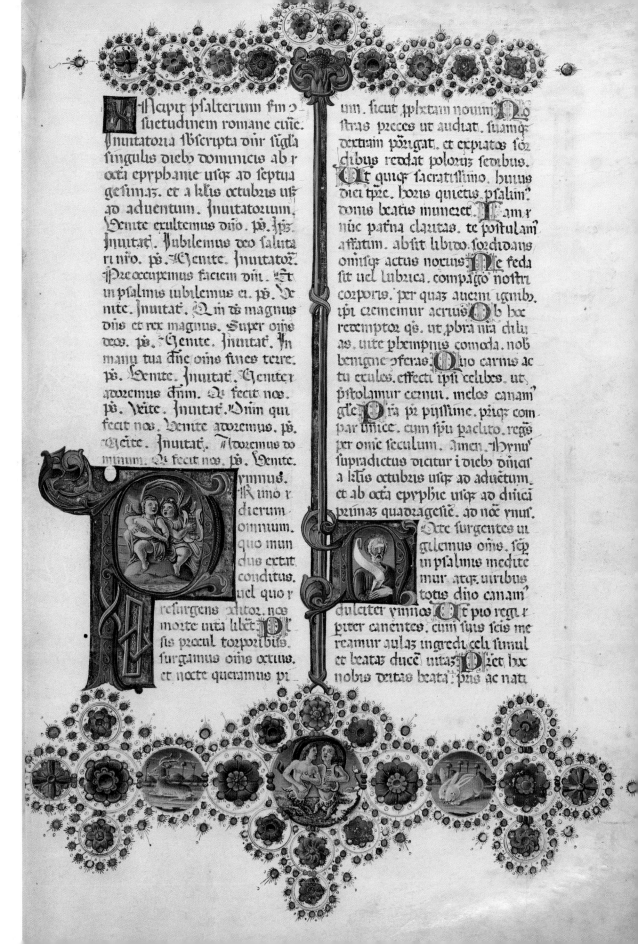

Incipit psalterium scdm con-
suetudinem romane curie.
Inuitatoria subscripta dnr sigla
singulis diebus dominicis ab r
octa epyphanie usqz ad septua
gesimaz. et a klis octubris us
ad aduentum. Inuitatorium.
Venite exultemus dno. ps. xciiii.
Inuitat. Iubilemus deo saluta
ri nro. ps. Venite. Inuitatoz.
Preoccupemus faciem dni. Et
in psalmis iubilemus ei. ps. Ve
nite. Inuitat. Qm ds magnus
dns et rex magnus. Super omes
deos. ps. Venite. Inuitat. In
manu tua dne omis fines terre.
ps. Venite. Inuitat. Venite
adoremus dnm. Qi fecit nos.
ps. Veite. Inuitat. Onim qui
fecit nos. Venite adoremus. ps.
Venite. Inuitat. Adoremus do
minum. Qi fecit nos. ps. Venite.
Hymnus.

Primo r
dierum
omnium.
quo mun
dus extat
conditus.
uel quo r
resurgens xptor. nos
morte victa liberat. Pul
sis procul torporibus.
surgamus omis ocius.
et nocte queramus pi

um. sicut ppletam nouim. No
stras preces ut audiat. suamqz
dexteram porrigat. et expiatos sor
dibus reddat polorum sedibus.
Ut quiqz sacratissimo. huius
diei tpre. horis quietis psallim.
donis beatis munerer. Iam r
nunc paterna claritas. te postulam
affatim. absit libido sordidans
omisqz actus noxius. Ne feda
sit uel lubrica. compago nostri
corporis. per quaz auerni ignibus.
ipsi cremenur acrius. Ob hoc
redemptor qs. ut probra nra dilu
as. uite perhennis comoda. nob
benigne conferas. Quo carnis ac
tu exules. effecti ipsi celibes. ut
pstolamur cernui. melos canam
glie. Presta pr pyssime. patrqz com
par unice. cum spu paclito. regns
per omne seculum. amen. Hymnus
supradictus dicitur i diebus dnicis
a klis octubris usqz ad aduentum.
et ab octa epyphie usqz ad dnica
primaz quadragesie. ad noct ymur.

Nocte surgentes ui
gilemus omis. sep
in psalmis medite
mur atqz uiribus
totis dno canam
dulciter ymnos Ut pio regi r
piter canentes. cum suis scis me
reamur aulas ingredi celi simul
et beatas ducere uitas Psit hoc
nobis deitas beata. patris ac nati

וְאֵלֶּה שְׁמוֹת בְּנֵי יִשְׂרָאֵל הַבָּאִים מִצְרָיְמָה אֵת יַעֲקֹב אִישׁ וּבֵיתוֹ בָּאוּ ׀
רְאוּבֵן שִׁמְעוֹן לֵוִי וִיהוּדָה ׀ יִשָּׂשכָר זְבוּלֻן וּבִנְיָמִן ׀
דָּן וְנַפְתָּלִי גָּד וְאָשֵׁר ׀ וַיְהִי כָּל־נֶפֶשׁ יֹצְאֵי יֶרֶךְ־יַעֲקֹב שִׁבְעִים נָפֶשׁ וְיוֹסֵף הָיָה בְמִצְרָיִם ׀ וַיָּמָת יוֹסֵף וְכָל־אֶחָיו וְכֹל הַדּוֹר הַהוּא ׀ וּבְנֵי יִשְׂרָאֵל פָּרוּ וַיִּשְׁרְצוּ וַיִּרְבּוּ וַיַּעַצְמוּ בִּמְאֹד מְאֹד וַתִּמָּלֵא הָאָרֶץ אֹתָם ׀

וַיָּקָם מֶלֶךְ־חָדָשׁ עַל־מִצְרָיִם אֲשֶׁר לֹא־יָדַע אֶת־יוֹסֵף ׀ וַיֹּאמֶר אֶל־עַמּוֹ הִנֵּה עַם בְּנֵי יִשְׂרָאֵל רַב וְעָצוּם מִמֶּנּוּ ׀ הָבָה נִתְחַכְּמָה לוֹ פֶּן־יִרְבֶּה וְהָיָה כִּי־תִקְרֶאנָה מִלְחָמָה וְנוֹסַף גַּם־הוּא עַל־שֹׂנְאֵינוּ וְנִלְחַם־בָּנוּ וְעָלָה מִן־הָאָרֶץ ׀ וַיָּשִׂימוּ עָלָיו שָׂרֵי מִסִּים לְמַעַן עַנֹּתוֹ בְּסִבְלֹתָם וַיִּבֶן עָרֵי מִסְכְּנוֹת לְפַרְעֹה אֶת־פִּתֹם וְאֶת־רַעַמְסֵס ׀ וְכַאֲשֶׁר יְעַנּוּ אֹתוֹ כֵּן יִרְבֶּה וְכֵן יִפְרֹץ וַיָּקֻצוּ מִפְּנֵי בְּנֵי יִשְׂרָאֵל ׀ וַיַּעֲבִדוּ מִצְרַיִם אֶת־בְּנֵי יִשְׂרָאֵל בְּפָרֶךְ ׀ וַיְמָרְרוּ אֶת־חַיֵּיהֶם בַּעֲבֹדָה קָשָׁה בְּחֹמֶר וּבִלְבֵנִים וּבְכָל־עֲבֹדָה בַּשָּׂדֶה אֵת כָּל־עֲבֹדָתָם אֲשֶׁר־עָבְדוּ בָהֶם בְּפָרֶךְ ׀ וַיֹּאמֶר מֶלֶךְ מִצְרַיִם לַמְיַלְּדֹת הָעִבְרִיֹּת אֲשֶׁר שֵׁם הָאַחַת שִׁפְרָה וְשֵׁם הַשֵּׁנִית פּוּעָה ׀ וַיֹּאמֶר בְּיַלֶּדְכֶן אֶת־הָעִבְרִיּוֹת וּרְאִיתֶן עַל־הָאָבְנָיִם אִם־בֵּן הוּא וַהֲמִתֶּן אֹתוֹ וְאִם־בַּת הִוא

illumination flourished. The most renowned artist who took residence in Ferrara under Borso's rule was Taddeo Crivelli, who introduced the Renaissance style into manuscript painting in Ferrara. His first known miniatures date to the early 1450s. In the period roughly coinciding with the rule of Borso d'Este over Ferrara, Crivelli and his workshop were engaged in a number of projects, producing a variety of books for aristocratic patrons as well as for religious institutions and individuals. Two manuscripts of undisputed Ferrarese origin may serve as examples. The first is a breviary made in 1470 for Johannes Baptista de Girardis of Bologna, canon of St Peter's in Rome. The canon must have had his liturgical duties in mind when he commissioned this huge manuscript of 35 cm × 28 cm × 10 cm (figure 33). Crivelli's most important commission was the costly and magnificent Bible of Borso d'Este, one of the greatest achievements of Italian manuscript illumination. It took him and his team six years, from 1455 to 1461, to decorate this large, two-volume work, now in the Biblioteca Estense di Modena (Lat. 429).[6] Crivelli left Ferrara shortly after the death of Duke Borso in 1471.

Before turning to MS. Canon. Or. 62 it should be noticed that the Jews were welcomed in Ferrara throughout the fifteenth century and gained ducal protection. Due to the policy of the d'Este family to strengthen the economy there was a growing need for credit, which facilitated the settlement of Jews. They were probably at first admitted as money-lenders, though they afterwards became active as retailers, manufacturers and tradesmen. It therefore may well be that certain members of the Jewish community in Ferrara in the second half of the fifteenth century could afford to commission a lavishly illuminated manuscript such as Canon. Or. 62.[7]

When compared with the breviary produced in 1470 for the canon in Rome the strong similarity between the two manuscripts cannot easily be overlooked. The use of the very specific floral illuminations, characteristic of the Ferrarese school of painting, is a strong indication that our Hebrew codex has, as with the breviary, Ferrara as its artistic birthplace (figure 34). Other illuminations such as rabbits and deer – though very common as illustrations – show such similarity that they may originate from the same artistic school. Colours and background of these images being very similar are further confirmation that the wealthy Jew had his manuscript illuminated in a Christian workshop in Ferrara, used by the clergy and the Duke himself (figure 35).

Most intriguing, however, is the image of the unicorn, a mythical creature which was part of the crest of the d'Este family. That Borso chose it as his personal emblem, which embellished the monumental main doorway of the Palazzo Schifanoia, may be explained by the fact

Figure 34 *left*
Pentateuch with Haftarot and Megillot: beginning of the book of Exodus (Northern Italy [Ferrara?], 1472). Oxford, Bodleian Library, MS. Canon. Or. 62, fol. 47r.

Figure 35 *above*
top Oxford, Bodleian Library, MS. Canon. Lit. 383, fol. 7r, detail.
bottom Oxford, Bodleian Library, MS. Canon. Or. 62, fol. 47r, detail.

that he was an illegitimate son in the family. The unicorn could well have been a way of legitimizing the interruption of the hereditary line of succession. In the bibbia di Borso the unicorn is depicted twice in exactly the same way as on the façade of the Palazzo Schifanoia: piercing his horn into the water. The image is a symbol of taming the waters, one of the many qualities ascribed to the unicorn, here applied to Borso's involvement in canalization and irrigation projects in the Val Padana, the alluvial plain of the Po river valley.[8]

The fact that the unicorn is part of the illumination of our manuscript links it closely to the Ferrarese artistic tradition, but the actual portrayal gives it undoubtedly a different meaning. We see here the unicorn portrayed in the lap of the virgin, an image that unmistakably bears a Christological significance found already in Patristic literature (figure 36). In his comment on Deut. 33: 17 'His [Joseph's] glory is like the firstling of his bullock, and his horns are like the horns of the wild ox [the unicorn]; with them he shall push the people together to the ends of the earth' the early Christian writer Tertullian (c. 160–c. 220) points to the Christological meaning of the unicorn explaining that 'this animal signifies Christ and the horn denotes Christ's cross.'[9] It is this Christological claim encompassing Christ's Incarnation and Passion which the unicorn in late medieval Christian iconography represents. Medieval manuscripts occasionally focus on one of these two components, which form the inclusion of Christ's redemptive activity. The unicorn depicted with its forefeet in the lap of the virgin in the Book of Hours, probably produced in Delft (Netherlands) around 1470, is part of a broader scene which shows the Holy Family fleeing Herod, who is planning to kill the newly born king–Messiah (figure 37). The image of the unicorn here focuses on the incarnation of Christ.

In the Ormesby Psalter (Oxford, Bodleian Library, MS. Douce 366), one of the most magnificent of English fourteenth-century manuscripts, it is Christ's passion which is the theme of the illumination, intimately related to the text of Psalm 22 according to the Vulgate. In the passion stories of the New Testament the psalm functions as road map and was therefore always understood as predicting Jesus' crucifixion. The miniature in the main initial of the psalm shows us Jesus before Pilate and the unicorn at the bottom of the page functions as a metaphor for the trial of Jesus (figure 38). The Roman soldier plunging his spear into the unicorn means to remind us of the scene at the cross in the gospel of John, where a soldier pierced Jesus' side with a spear (19: 34).

There is one other element of this illuminated page that requires our attention in the context of the unicorn. In the secular bestiary

Figure 36 *left*
Beginning of the book of Genesis. Oxford, Bodleian Library, MS. Canon. Or. 62, fol. 1r.

Figure 37 *pp. 64–5*
Unicorn in a Book of Hours from Delft (Netherlands), second quarter of the fifteenth century. Oxford, Bodleian Library, MS. Douce 248, fols 127v–128r.

Hier beghinnen die corte ghetiden
van onser liever vrouwen marie
Metten hoe si wort ontfaen
Daer om se salich iet lach aen
Maria maghet ontfaet dat v van
den here biden enghel ouerghesent
is. Maria labia mea aperies Eros

rouwe doet
op mine lip
pen. En min
mout sel voer
kunghe dyn
lof die soet is
Maria druc

ke te miinre hulpe. Maria haest
v om te helpen. Glorie si den va
der ende den sone en den halighen
gheest Alst was inden beghi

te deploramus: ualeamus euincere in
sultationes aduersantium uitiorum. per
in custodiam uias
meas: ut non delin
quam in lingua me
a. Posui ori meo cu
stodiam: cum con
sisteret aduersum me.
Obmutui et humiliatus sum et silui a bo
nis: et dolor meus renouatus est
Concaluit cor meum intra me: et in me
ditatione mea exardescet ignis.
Locutus sum in lingua mea: notum fac
michi domine finem meum.
Et numerum dierum meorum qui est:
ut sciam quid desit michi.
Ecce mensurabiles posuisti dies meos:
et substantia mea tamquam nichilum ante te

narrative the unicorn and the virgin are part of a hunting scene in which the hunters try in vain to seize the unicorn, but which can only be captured when, enthralled by the virgin, it springs into her lap and embraces her. In medieval Christian iconography all aspects of the hunting scene were given a symbolic meaning. Not only the virgin and the unicorn but also the hunters and their dogs figure in the Christological interpretation, particularly when the narrative is applied to Jesus' Passion. Psalm 22 lends itself to such an application. Intimately related to v. 16 'For dogs encompass me; a company of evildoers encircles me' and v. 20 'deliver my soul from the sword my precious life from the power of the dog', we find two dogs on either side of the psalm text representing Jesus' persecutors, who according to unanimous Christian tradition are the Jews (figure 39).[10]

The Jewish owner was probably not unfamiliar with the image of the unicorn, which is also a familiar Jewish symbol. As in Christian tradition it represents salvation, but then, of course, of Israel. And it is not only the redemptive meaning of the unicorn that is claimed by Christians and Jews alike, but also the unicorn as the victim of a hunt, which symbolizes for Christians Jesus' suffering at the hands of the Jews and for Jews Christians persecuting them. Here we see the role of persecutor and victim reversed.[11]

It should be noticed that in MS. Canon. Or. 62 the imagery is reduced to the virgin and the unicorn without any allusion to hunters or dogs. Since both Christians and Jews attributed the same meaning to the scene – that is, redemption – and made this an expression of their own beliefs and expectations, one could argue the image in MS. Canon. Or. 62 of the virgin and the unicorn may have been understood by the owner of the manuscript in a subversive way as the expression of his most fervent hope: the redemption of Israel.

There is, however, a final observation to be made. The image in MS. Canon. Or. 62 is unmistakably Christian. The unicorn appears at the beginning of Genesis, which recounts the story of Eve and her disobedience and transgression of God's directive not to eat of the tree of life. In Christian theology the disobedient Eve is counter-acted by Mary, who already in the early Church is portrayed as the second Eve just as Jesus is as the second Adam. The second Eve is the beginning of the second Creation or re-creation of humanity through Christ's redemption. The early church father Irenaeus (d. *c.* 202) in his *Adversus haereses* (3,22) initiated this theology and wrote: 'Mary the Virgin is found to be obedient, saying: "Behold, O Lord, your handmaid; be it done to me according to your word"[Luke 1:38] Eve, however, was disobedient.... Thus, the knot of Eve's disobedience was untied by the obedience of Mary. What the virgin Eve bound in

Figure 38 *left*
Ormesby Psalter: Roman soldier plunging his spear into the unicorn (England, fourteenth century). Oxford, Bodleian Library, MS. Douce 366, fol. 55v.

Figure 39 *above and below*
Ormesby Psalter: Dogs representing Jesus' persecutors. Oxford, Bodleian Library, MS. Douce 366, fol. 55v.

Figure 40
Adam and Eve. Virgin
with unicorn; Oxford,
Bodleian Library, MS.
Canon. Or. 62, fol. 1r.

unbelief, the Virgin Mary untied through faith' (figure 40). The theological dimension of the image of the unicorn set in this particular context does not allow the owner of the manuscript to appropriate it for his own hope and expectation. The owner could have erased the image from his handmade liturgy. In this particular case a Jew of Ferrara was content to follow the weekly reading of the Torah from a text which flaunted Christian beliefs.

NOTES

1. See the contribution by Eva Frojmovic in this volume.
2. See F. Madan, *A summary catalogue of Western manuscripts in the Bodleian Library at Oxford which have not hitherto been catalogued in the quarto series with references to the Oriental and other manuscripts.* Vol. IV (Oxford, 1897), 313–14.
3. MS. Canon. Or. 94: Seph. square script, Spain fourteenth century; MS. Opp. 14: Ashk. square and semi-cursive scripts, 1340 (figurative Masorah); MS. Opp. Add. 4° 47: Ashk. square and semi-cursive scripts, Ashkenaz early thirteenth century; MS. Canon. Or. 91: Ashk. square script, Ashkenaz 1305 (non-figurative Masorah); MS. Opp. 13: Ashk. square script, Ashkenaz 1302 (non-figurative Masorah); MS. Opp. Add. 4° 26: Seph. square script, Spain 1480; MS. Canon. Or. 42: Seph. square script, Moura (Portugal) 1470 (non-figurative Masorah); MS. Poc. 30: Seph. square script, Spain 1483 (initials coloured); MS. Canon. Or. 41: Seph. square script, Spain fourteenth century (primitive drawings); MS. Mich. 142: Seph. square script, Spain fourteenth–fifteenth century; MS. Canon. Or. 106: Seph.-Italian square script, Northern Italy 1500; MS. Opp. 15: Ashk. square script, Ashkenaz *c.* 1300; MS. Canon. Or. 77: Seph. square script, Berlanga (Spain) 1455 (decorative frames); MS. Mich. 628–629: Ashk. square script for biblical texts, cursive for Rashi, Ashkenaz late thirteenth century (non-figurative Masorah); MS. Marshall Or. 51: Ashk. square script for biblical texts, cursive for Rashi, France? second half thirteenth century.
4. See e.g. MS. Opp. 13, where the name Solomon is frequently pointed out in the Masorah (e.g. fols 33v, 162r, 439r) and MS. Mich. 629, where the name Joseph appears in decorated form on fol. 19r.
5. See M. Beit-Arié, *Catalogue of the Hebrew Manuscripts in the Bodleian Library: Supplement of Addenda and Corrigenda to Volume I (A. Neubauer's catalogue),* compiled under the direction of Malachi Beit-Arié, ed. R.A. May (Oxford, 1994), no. 26.
6. For a description of the bible, see A. Johnson Wright, *The Bible of Borso d'Este: Christian Piety and Political Rhetoric in Quattrocento Ferrara* (Ann Arbor, 2003), 2–15.
7. For the Jews in Ferrara, see A. Balletti, *Gli ebrei e gli Estensi* (Reggio Emilia, 1930).
8. See further Johnson Wright, *The Bible of Borso d'Este.*
9. See M.M. Epstein, *Dreams of Subversion in Medieval Jewish Art and Literature* (University Park, Penn., 1997), 150 n48.
10. For a full analysis of the manuscript see F.C.E. Law-Turner, *The Ormesby Psalter: An English Medieval Masterpiece* (Oxford, 2009).
11. For a thorough discussion of the various interpretations of the unicorn in Christian and Jewish tradition, see Epstein, *Dreams,* 96–112.

CHAPTER 6

The Oppenheimer Siddur: Artist and Scribe in a Fifteenth-century Hebrew Prayer Book

Suzanne Wijsman

The Manuscript

Ashkenazic Hebrew illuminated manuscripts reflect the intersection of Jewish and Christian cultures in medieval northern Europe in a variety of ways, including shared iconography and other aspects of production. A fifteenth-century Ashkenazic *siddur* (book of daily prayers) from the Oppenheimer collection in the Bodleian Library, MS. Opp. 776, stands out as an unusual example because not only is it dated and richly illuminated, but it was not produced on commission by a professional scribe: according to the colophon the copyist, Asher ben Isaac, made it for the use of his own family.[1] In the colophon, he states that he completed it on 1 Tammuz 5231 (28 June 1471). Although no specific location of production is mentioned, codicological features suggest German provenance because both sides of the fine parchment leaves have been scraped to achieve an equalized texture, a practice seen only in medieval Ashkenazic manuscripts made in Germany, mainly after 1300.[2] This manuscript is very small and therefore would have been highly portable.[3]

Although more than half of all dated medieval Hebrew manuscripts are assumed to have been copied by individuals for personal use, the number of such manuscripts from all regions that are illuminated is very small.[4] Among these user-produced manuscripts, the illumination and decoration of this prayer book make it exceptional. A wide range of richly coloured pigments has been used and there is evidence of generous use of gold leaf, occurring on all but three of the thirty-three illuminated folios. It has many finely drawn and painted illustrations, which include musicians, praying figures, hybrids, animals, birds, flowers, foliage and architectural motifs. In addition, many folios have sections often highlighted in decorative patterns such as alternating colours for words, letters or lines of text. All of this serves to attract the eye and enhance the readability of the texts.

The variety in style and size of scripts in the calligraphy is equally impressive, as well as the arrangement of texts into decorative shapes and their ornamentation. The scribe has used a variety of typical medieval Ashkenazic script types, such as square script for main titles and transitions, and Gothic semi-cursive script for subsidiary titles and main texts.[5] Using devices typical of Ashkenazic scribes, the scribe has been fastidious in the consistent justification of lines at the left margin or, in the case of final lines or words, centring these within text columns, in keeping with line management practices exhibited in many medieval Hebrew manuscripts.[6] This shows care and skill on the part of the scribe in achieving a pleasing appearance in the copied texts.[7] While the extensive use of gold leaf and variety of pigments are an indication of the material costs associated with the manuscript's production, the planning of the layout and attractive scribal work testify further to the investment of time made by this Ashkenazic owner–scribe in creating a beautiful *siddur* for his family to use.

Paradoxically, despite the scribe's meticulous approach to the visual presentation of texts and evidence of proofreading, seen in the many corrections he noted throughout the manuscript, the *siddur* contains a large number of copying errors. His tendency to make such mistakes – especially misplaced, repeated or wrong words which he sometimes corrected – suggests that Asher ben Isaac was not a professional scribe. In addition to copying errors, there are also textual variants as well as deviations from the standard liturgical rite, which may indicate that the scribe followed a different tradition.[8]

The Artwork

Over the past few decades there has been much discussion about the participation of Jewish and/or Christian artists in the production of medieval Hebrew illuminated manuscripts.[9] There is evidence in Hebrew manuscripts for the involvement of both Jewish and Christian artists in this process, and, unless the identity of the artist is specified in a colophon or indicated elsewhere, questions inevitably are reiterated in the case of each individual manuscript: was the artist Jewish or Christian or, as part of his commission for the copying work, did a Jewish scribe oversee and 'design' the artistic production which was then carried out by a Christian artist or workshop?[10]

The colophon of MS. Opp. 776 does not make clear who was responsible for the artwork in this *siddur*. However, because of its user-produced origins, this highly decorated and illuminated manuscript provides us with the opportunity to examine these questions from a different perspective. We know that there was no hypothetical 'middle man', a hired scribe, involved in the production of this prayer book. Without a presumed intermediary between patron and artist we can be confident, at the very least, that the way the texts are visually presented deliberately expresses the wishes of Asher ben Isaac, its scribe and owner. Moreover, two other aspects of the manuscript indicate that the subjects and motifs included in the artwork are the result of conscious choice and intentional planning on the part of the scribe. First, there are artistic and codicological features which, when examined together, constitute compelling evidence to suggest that the scribe was also the artist. Second, on some illuminated folios, texts and images are also noticeably connected.

There are questions concerning the sequence of production of MS. Opp. 776 in terms of the order of copying, drawing and painting, since several folios show script and underdrawings that are overlapping, or points of contact between paint and script.[11] With the naked eye, it is difficult to judge the sequence in which the execution of artwork and copying occurred because of the small size of the illustrations. A preliminary technical analysis carried out at the Bodleian Library suggests that planning and execution of underdrawings preceded scribal work on some folios, and provides confirmation that some painting occurred after copying.[12] If it is indeed the case that copying and application of pigments occurred after planning of the layout and the execution of drawings, this manuscript does not conform to the kind of sequential production seen in many other illuminated Hebrew manuscripts, where it is often obvious that drawings and painting have been done after the main texts were copied.[13] Rather, it suggests that copying and artwork may have been done concurrently.

Even more notable are decorative elements in the text, such as ornamented letters and marginal flourishes, that are a feature of Asher ben Isaac's scribal practice but that also appear in the painted illuminations. Such decorative scribal embellishments are common in Hebrew manuscripts, and the individuality of these devices helps to characterize the unique hand of each scribe.[14] In MS. Opp. 776, a filigree flourish appears frequently in the margins as a means of highlighting the beginnings of text lines. We are certain this was done during the copying process, since it occurs at the beginnings and endings of lines and in the same ink colour as that of successive or preceding letters, or in a contrasting colour where an alternating colour pattern occurs in the texts.[15] The most elaborate example of this is found on fol. 77v (figure 41), where the filigree pattern is combined with another recurring motif: a stylized, quarter-sectioned

Figure 41 *right*
Oppeheimer Siddur.
Oxford, Bodleian Library,
MS. Opp. 776, fol. 77v.

Figure 42 *below*
Oppeheimer Siddur.
Oxford, Bodleian Library,
MS. Opp. 776, fol. 33v.

floret. These have been done using a quill in the same blue ink used in the copying of the coloured texts that conclude this section of the Yom Kippur prayers.[16] The florets and filigree pattern here have a distinctive identifiable style.

It is significant, therefore, that these two motifs reappear throughout the manuscript separately or combined, using pigments that also occur in the illuminations and in colours that are different from those of the inks used for the script. For example, on fol. 33v (figure 42) the colours used for the red floret and green filigree foliage match those in the green border with a red dot pattern and the red crest on the left-hand bird's head. The style and shape of both florets and filigree foliage – here executed

with a brush rather than a quill – are strik-
ingly similar to those on fol. 77v.

Filigree and florets also appear
independently, as component parts of word
panel illuminations. In particular, filigree in
the same style appears as background filler
on many illuminated panels in a variety
of different colours, including distinctive
pigments that have also been used for the
painted illuminations. For example, the panel
for the beginning of the Hallel (Psalms 113–118)
on fol. 45v (figure 43) has filigree decoration
in a linenfold banner using the same deep
blue pigment as in the background painting
of the panel. By contrast, on fol. 65v (figure
44) we find a light blue pigment used both in
copying and decoration all on the same page:
in ornamental filigree, as the panel background colour, and for an
initial word.

Filigree that has been rendered with a distinctive red-orange
pigment appears as filler in the background of two panels (e.g. fol.
74r, figure 45). This colour is found in many of the finest details in
the painting and decoration of panels in the *siddur* where the artist
uses it to achieve the effect of light and shade, for example, on the
folds of the red-toned garment worn by one of the musicians on fol.
79v (figures 46 and 47). Hence, it is clear that this is a pigment from
the artist's palette. These are but a few examples of the way in which

Figure 43
Oppeheimer Siddur.
Oxford, Bodleian Library,
MS. Opp. 776, fol. 45v.

Figure 44
Oppeheimer Siddur.
Oxford, Bodleian Library,
MS. Opp. 776, fol. 65v.

Figure 45 *right*
Oppeheimer Siddur.
Oxford, Bodleian Library,
MS. Opp. 776, fol. 74r.

Figure 46 *below*
Oppeheimer Siddur.
Oxford, Bodleian Library,
MS. Opp. 776, fol. 79v.

this filigree motif has been used in the decoration scheme. The close stylistic relationship of filigree decoration in panel illuminations and scribal flourishes leads to the inescapable conclusion that all were executed by one hand, that of the scribe–artist, Asher ben Isaac.

One other clue points to the probability that Asher ben Isaac was the artist. The floret motif, noted above, occurs not only as part of the painted decoration and scribal ornamentation, but also in two word panels as five-pointed florets that have been drawn, gilded and outlined at the same time as the Hebrew titles (e.g. fol. 62r, figure 48).[17] It would be easy to assume that Asher ben Isaac used this merely as a graphic filler to avoid leftover space in the word panel due to a miscalculation in planning the space needed for a short initial word, or that it is a decorative ornament bearing no special significance. However, the regular occurrence of four- and five-petalled florets at many points in the manuscript suggests that this motif was deliberately selected. The inclusion of florets in two gilded initial word panels – which were undoubtedly executed by the scribe – suggests that this motif could have had some kind of emblematic significance.

Figure 47
Oppeheimer Siddur.
Oxford, Bodleian Library,
MS. Opp. 776, fol. 79v.

Artists' working materials such as pigments and models, as well as sophisticated painting techniques, were clearly available to this scribe–artist. The artist's training and professional competence is seen in the subtle use of pigments to create light and shade, as noted above (figure 46), and in the expressive and detailed rendering of faces, bodies and hand gestures of the numerous human and hybrid figures, especially the musicians. The application of gold leaf was less successful and perhaps less expertly done, showing many areas where the gold has failed to adhere to the binder despite an obvious attempt to achieve a brilliant effect with so much gold leaf applied to initial words and illustrations.

The Iconography

The presence of many performing musicians, such as the group of nine depicted on fol. 79v (figures 46 and 47), is the most prominent theme in the iconography of this manuscript. Musicians appear from the first illuminated folio (fol. 2r, figure 49) to the last (fol. 89r, figure 50). Not only are there a larger number of musicians than in any other extant illuminated Hebrew manuscript (forty-four), but they are shown playing at least ten types of instruments which are known to have been commonly used by instrumentalists and minstrels during the late Middle Ages.[18] The instruments include both loud (*haut*) and soft (*bas*) instruments. The loud instruments are: the bagpipe, horn (shofar), an instrument that is probably a shawm, a straight trumpet-like instrument with a narrowly flared bell played one-handed,[19] and

Figure 48
Oppeheimer Siddur.
Oxford, Bodleian Library,
MS. Opp. 776, fol. 62r.

a brass instrument that is probably a folded trumpet, held horizontally and to the side.[20] The soft instruments are: a small-waisted fiddle, the lute and gittern, medieval harp, duct flute (or pipe), and *portativ* organ.[21] It is worth noting that the instruments in the illuminations of MS. Opp. 776 sometimes appear in ensemble combinations popular in the fifteenth century, such as the pairing of lute and fiddle. Keith Polk's work on fifteenth-century German civic payment records reveals that this string duo was one of the most common instrumental combinations of the period.[22] The Jewish *Tanzhaus* (dance house) provided one venue for activity by Ashkenazic Jewish musicians, but employment was found also outside the Jewish community.[23] It is thus likely that these were some of the instruments used by Jewish and Christian musicians alike.

A high level of executant skill would have been needed for the artist to render these tiny figures with such detail and individuality, and an awareness of actual musical practice or access to excellent models to represent elements of performance. For example, the lute and gittern players are all shown with opposing plucking thumb and fingers, probably indicating the use of a plectrum, as is typical in other depictions of lutenists from this period, such as we see on fol. 79v (figure 51).[24]

Another notable feature of this manuscript's artwork are links with fifteenth-century German engravings in some illuminations. For example, this manuscript shows strong affinities with early engraved playing cards and derivative copies. Such engravings were disseminated widely and probably used as model sheets throughout Europe

Figure 49
Oppeheimer Siddur.
Oxford, Bodleian Library,
MS. Opp. 776, fol. 2r.

during the fifteenth century. Evidence for the use of such models in Hebrew manuscripts is not new; this phenomenon was first noted by Sheila Edmunds in the late 1970s.[25] What is interesting about their appearance in this *siddur* is that some of the animals and birds more closely resemble figures in the earliest versions of the cards, such as those by the Master of the Playing Cards, than similar figures in some other Hebrew manuscripts made at about the same time.[26] For example, the angry blue swan on fol. 57r (figure 52) and the crested bird on fol. 33v (figure 42) are both close matches for birds found on the Six of Birds card by the Master of the Playing Cards (figure 53).

Relationship of Texts and Images

The significance of Asher ben Isaac's creation of this manuscript is seen not only in the copying and fine artwork of the *siddur*, but also in his choice of subjects and motifs for the illustrations. One of the manuscript's most striking illuminations contains an image of nine

wild men in battle with clubs and contemporary medieval weapons, such as the dagger and bow-and-arrow (fol. 24v, figure 54). The dramatic violence and blood-red hue of the background in this illuminated panel, beginning the penitential prayers of the Tahanun for Mondays and Thursdays, are visually arresting and contrast starkly with the pretty painted miniatures that characterize the artwork of this manuscript

Figure 50 *far left*
Oppeheimer Siddur.
Oxford, Bodleian Library,
MS. Opp. 776, fol. 89r.

Figure 51 *left*
Oppeheimer Siddur.
Oxford, Bodleian Library,
MS. Opp. 776, fol. 79v.

Figure 52 *below*
Oppeheimer Siddur.
Oxford, Bodleian Library,
MS. Opp. 776, fol. 57r.

in general. The opposition on this page between the brown, ugly wild men in the main panel filling the top half of the page and the colourful musicians in the margins below underscores the striking quality of this illumination. The prayers of the Tahanun concern mourning the exile and the destruction of the Temple, and contain prayers for forgiveness from sin, redemption and the gathering of the Jewish people from among the gentiles.

This illustration of wild men is unprecedented in Hebrew manuscript art.[27] The violent scene here suggests that the artist knew both the form of the wild man as it appeared elsewhere in fifteenth-century German art and the nuances in meaning his image could convey. This applies particularly to iconographic conventions of the mythical wild man as a debased anti-social figure who, in the medieval hierarchy, was closer in his physiognomy and behaviour to animals than to that of men.[28] The spatial opposition between the wild men in the main panel and the musicians in the outer margins suggests that these are deliberately contrasting elements, a phenomenon noted in other medieval Ashkenazic

Figure 53
Six of Birds, engraving by
the Master of the Playing
Cards. Paris, Bibliothèque
Nationale.

Figure 54
Oppeheimer Siddur.
Oxford, Bodleian Library,
MS. Opp. 776, fol. 24v.

manuscripts by Sarit Shalev-Eyni.[29] In the context of the Tahanun, Asher ben Isaac's adaptation of the wild men motif invites an interpretation that in their violent behaviour here they symbolize gentiles (*goyim*). By contrast, the musicians throughout this manuscript are associated with sections of the liturgy dealing with worship, rejoicing and praise of God.[30]

Finally, although numerous motifs in this manuscript are shared with contemporaneous Christian religious and secular art, Jewish iconographic traditions are also represented. This is most evident in the three illuminations depicting groups of men at prayer.[31] The illustration on fol. 20v (figure 55) shows that the artist had knowledge of a specific Jewish ritual custom. Two bearded figures – both in red symmetrically placed in the group of seven praying men – are depicted in a way which clearly shows that their *tallit*, or prayer shawl, has been thrown over their left shoulder.[32] Two corners of the *tallit* are visible on the front of the left-hand figure with the rest of the *tallit* draped over his shoulder, falling at the back. He is resting his cheek on his right hand, perhaps in a gesture of mourning – a motif which appears in two other illustrations in this manuscript and may be connected with a long iconographic tradition of mourning gestures in Christian religious art.[33] The right-hand figure also has the *tallit* thrown over his left shoulder.

Amos Geula has discussed this manner of throwing the *tallit* as a custom practised in earlier medieval times by the pietist group Hasidei Ashkenaz.[34] Geula's research has shown that the custom of throwing the *tallit* was not widely practised in Ashkenaz and even was condemned in some medieval Jewish sources. In this illustration, marking one of the most important daily prayers (the Amidah), the artist has chosen to combine the depiction of this distinctive Jewish ritual custom with a mourning gesture also seen widely in medieval Christian religious art.

Conclusion

The foregoing discussion points to the conclusion that Asher ben Isaac was both artist and copyist of MS. Opp. 776. In this outstanding and beautiful example of a decorated and illuminated medieval Hebrew book we see the

Figure 55
Oppeheimer Siddur.
Oxford, Bodleian Library,
MS. Opp. 776, fol. 20v.

engagement of a Jewish scribe–artist with the visual culture of his time and place.[35] This is shown materially in his use of contemporary models, motifs and specialized techniques in the execution of the artwork, and conceptually in the contextualization of images with which he has chosen to mark titles and transition points for the texts in his *siddur*. Living and working in fifteenth-century Germany, Asher ben Isaac drew on a repertoire of motifs that were current in his day, reflecting both Jewish and Christian iconographic traditions.

Furthermore, whilst we can hardly assume that the illuminations in MS. Opp. 776 portray actual performers, since the musicians in the *siddur* have a symbolic rather than representational function in relation to the texts, the unusually large number and quality of the illustrations of musicians makes it an important source for musical iconography among medieval Hebrew manuscripts. Given the convergence of this central musical theme with the manuscript's genesis as a user-produced book, it is tempting to speculate that the pervasive musical iconography of this manuscript may have been personally meaningful for Asher ben Isaac, since we know that Jewish instrumentalists worked both inside and outside the Jewish community during this period.[36] This is underscored by the fact that twelve of the twenty playful and animated figures drawn inside the outlines of Hebrew letters on the final illuminated page (fol. 89r, figure 50) are shown with many of the same instruments that appear throughout the *siddur*. This folio does not contain liturgical texts, but rather presents an abbreviated conventional ending formula, which Asher ben Isaac has chosen to decorate in this elaborate way.[37] These master-fully executed and charming drawings, immediately preceding the colophon on fol. 90r, thus provide a whimsical but virtuosic coda which concludes the manuscript's artwork.

This all implies a level of interaction with the surrounding culture on the part of this fifteenth-century Jewish scribe–artist beyond that sanctioned by ecclesiastical or civic statutes of medieval Christian society. Through the personal choices he made in its production, we are afforded a refracted glimpse of his world-view. As such, this remarkable small prayer book made by a man for his family is more than a testament to fatherly love and religious devotion.

NOTES

1. Colophon translation: 'I finished this prayer on the first day of the fourth month in the 231st year in the sixth millennium, according to the Creation era [1 Tammuz, 5231 or 28 June, 1471]. I am Asher ben Rabbi Isaac who requests this. It is my wish that my sons and the sons of my sons will pray to God with it. And my soul desires and watches for the coming of the Redeemer. Make us powerful and strong in the building of the Temple. Grant peace, make fruitful and be pleased with all your servants. And show the rest of my brothers, your people Israel, peace.' I am indebted to Malachi Beit-Arié for his generous help and support for this research, including providing information from SfarData, the codicological database of the Hebrew Palaeography Project of the Israel Academy of Sciences and Humanities.

2. M. Beit-Arié, *Hebrew Codicology: Tentative Typology of Technical Practices Employed in Hebrew Dated Medieval Manuscripts*, (Jerusalem, 1981), 22–6.

3. Average folio size approx. 94 × 82 mm. These dimensions do not reflect the original size as the manuscript was badly trimmed at some stage so that the decorated space and illuminations of some folia are cut off.

4. A search of SfarData has revealed only sixteen dated user-produced or undestined manuscripts from all regions. On user-produced Hebrew books, see M. Beit-Arié, *Hebrew Manuscripts of East and West: Towards a Comparative Codicology – The Panizzi Lectures 1992* (London, 1992), 14–15 and 79–83; 'Transmission of Texts by Scribes and Copyists: Unconscious and Critical Interferences', *Bulletin of the John Rylands University Library of Manchester* 75:3 (1993), 33–52, esp. 39–46; *Unveiled Faces of Medieval Hebrew Books: The Evolution of Manuscript Production – Progression or Regression?* (Jerusalem, 2003), 62.

5. Smaller Ashkenazic semi-cursive and cursive scripts are used for refrains, congregational prayers, instructions to the reader and corrections. See the essay by M. Beit-Arié in this volume on Hebrew script types.

6. These include graphic fillers, letter dilation and constriction, anticipating letters, vertical insertions, placement of exceeding letters in the margins and abbreviated words. On line management devices in Hebrew manuscripts, see Beit-Arié, *Unveiled Faces*, 33–48.

7. For further discussion of functionality and aesthetics in medieval Hebrew manuscript production practices, see Beit-Arié, *Unveiled Faces*, 31.

8. This *siddur* offers a rich source for textual study in its halakhic and liturgical contents, which have yet to be comprehensively examined. The prayers represent the Western branch of the Ashkenazic rite (the rite used west of the River Elbe, sometimes characterized as Rhenish), but according to Dr N. Weissenstern of the Institute of Microfilmed Hebrew Manuscripts at the Jewish and National University Library there are also variants not seen elsewhere: the Av Ha-Rahamim prayers for those martyred during the Crusades recited on Sabbaths and holidays after the Torah reading (39v) has additions not found in the usual version. I am indebted to Dr Weissenstern for undertaking a preliminary analysis of this manuscript's liturgical texts and providing this information in private correspondence.

9. On the subject of Jewish and Christian art and artists/illuminators, see: B. Narkiss, *Hebrew Illuminated Manuscripts* (Jerusalem, 1969), 14–16; L. Mortara-Ottolenghi, 'The Illumination and the Artists', in *The Rothschild Miscellany* vol. II (London, 1989), 127–252; M. Beit-Arié, 'The Rothschild Miscellany', in *The Makings of the Medieval Hebrew Book* (Jerusalem, 1993), 181–90; Y. Zirlin, 'Joel Meets Joahannes: A Fifteenth-Century Jewish-Christian Collaboration in Manuscript Illumination', *Viator* 26 (1995), 265–82; M.M. Epstein, *Dreams of Subversion in Medieval Jewish Art and Literature* (University Park, Pa., 1997), 1–15; K. Kogman-Appel, 'Coping with Christian Pictorial Sources: What Did Jewish Miniaturists Not Paint?', *Speculum* 75:4 (2000), 816–58; S. Shalev-Eyni, 'Humor and Criticism: Christian Secular and Jewish Art of the Fourteenth Century', *Zeitschrift für Kunstgeschichte* 71 (2008), 188–206; *Jews Among Christians: A Hebrew School of Illumination of the Lake Constance Region* (Turnhout, 2009).

10. K. Kogman-Appel uses the term 'designer' to describe the hypothetical role of Jewish scribes in determining the subject content of illuminations, in her book *Illuminated Haggadot from Medieval Spain: Biblical Imagery and the Passover Holiday* (University Park, Pa., 2006), 12–13.

11. Examples occur, among others, on fols 35r, 57r and 62.

12. I am grateful to Sarah Neate of the Conservation Department of the Bodleian Library for carrying out a preliminary examination of the manuscript using binocular light microscopy, high-resolution digital photography and FTIR spectroscopy to assist in resolving some of these issues concerning MS. Opp. 776, and sharing this information with me, which comprises research for her D.Phil. thesis.

13. Copying has been completed but the artwork left unfinished in numerous examples of Hebrew manuscripts, e.g. Hamburg Staats- und Universitätsbibliothek Cod. hebr. 37 and British Library MS Add. 26954. On the unfinished artwork in a Hebrew manuscript, see also E.M. Cohen, 'Prato Haggadah', in Melanie Holcomb, ed., *Pen and Parchment: Drawing in the Middle Ages* (New York, 2009), 126–7.

14. For a more comprehensive discussion of para-scriptural and peri-textual elements in Hebrew manuscripts, see Beit-Arié, *The Makings of the Medieval Hebrew Book*, 78–92, and *Unveiled Faces*, 49–51.

15. The single exception to this is on fol. 1r where two ornamental flourishes have been added at the end of each text column using a distinctly different ink colour, suggesting that they were added later, possibly by the scribe.

16. It is clear from several points of overlapping pigments that coloured copying was done sequentially rather than concurrently: on this folio blue over red, suggesting that all the copying work in each ink colour was done at one time.

17. A third illuminated panel has a fleur-de-lis, another ornamental motif which occurs often in the artwork.

18. The musical iconography of MS. Opp. 776 will be treated in greater detail in a separate forthcoming article.

19. This instrument appears twice: on fols 30r and 48r.

20. I am grateful to Dr Jeremy Montagu for his observations concerning the identification of the wind instruments.

21. Two different sizes of plucked instruments appear to be depicted in MS. Opp. 776: the larger lute, which is shown with six strings and pegs, e.g. fols 6v and 79v, and a smaller instrument which more closely resembles the fifteenth-century gittern, e.g. fols 41v, 72v–73r.

22. For a discussion of German string playing during this era, see K. Polk, 'Vedel and Geige – Fiddle and Viol: German String Traditions in the Fifteenth Century', *Journal of the American Musicological Society* 42:3 (1989), 504–46.

23. W. Salmen, *Jüdische Musikanten und Tänzer vom 13. bis 20. Jahrhundert* (Innsbruck, 1991); 'Klezmer in Schlesien', *Musik des Ostens* 12 (1991), 283–6; 'Jüdische Hochzeits- und Tanzhäuser im Mittelalter', *Aschkenas* 5:1 (1995), 107–20; 'Der Juden Tanzhaus im Mittelalter', *Freiburger Rundbrief* NF 4 (Jg.4) (1997), 92–101.

24. For comparison with instruments in late-fifteenth-century Christian art, see J. Montagu, 'Musical Instruments in Hans Memling's Paintings', *Early Music* 35:4 (2007), 505–23, esp. figs 1,2, 4, and 13.

25. See S. Edmunds, 'A Note on the Art of Joseph Ibn Hayyim', *Studies in Bibliography and Booklore* 11:1–2 (1975/76), 25–40; 'The Kennicott Bible and the Use of Prints in Hebrew Manuscripts', in *Le stampe e la diffusione delle immagini e degli stili* Atti del XXIV Congresso C.I.H.A., 1979 (Bologna, 1980); K. Kogman-Appel, *Die Zweite Nürnberger und die Jehuda Haggada* (Frankfurt, 1999), 156–65; Mortara-Ottolenghi, *The Rothschild Miscellany*, 141.

26. For example, in the Kennicott Bible the playing-card motifs are closer in form and style to prints by the Master of the Power of Women. See Edmunds, 'A Note on the Art of Joseph Ibn Hayyim', 34.

27. A more complete discussion of wild men in Hebrew manuscript art will be presented in my forthcoming article, 'Wild Men, Musicians and Others in Hebrew Manuscript Art of the Middle Ages'.

28. For a more comprehensive discussion of the iconography of wild men, see: R. Bernheimer, *Wild Men in the Middle Ages: A Study in Art, Sentiment, and Demonology* (New York, 1970); E. Dudley and M.E. Novak, *The Wild Man Within* (Pittsburgh, 1972); T. Husband, *Wild Men in the Middle Ages: Medieval Myth and Symbolism* (New York, 1980); R. Bartra, *Wild Men in the Looking Glass* (Ann Arbor, 1994); G. Mobley, 'The Wild Man in the Bible and Ancient Near East', *Journal of Biblical Literature* 116:2 (1997), 217–33.

29. On redefining the relationship between 'model' and 'anti-model' and images in the centre and margins in Hebrew manuscript art, see S. Shalev-Eyni, 'Obvious and Ambiguous in Hebrew Illuminated Manuscripts from France and Germany', *Materia giudaica* 7:2 (2002), 249–71; *Jews Among Christians*, ch. 3.

30. For example, fol. 6v, the beginning of the *Pesuqei dezimira* (Verses of Praise), 8v for Psalm 19, and 12v for the beginning of the *Ashrei*.

31. Fols 8v, 20v and 83r.

32. I am indebted to Dr Amos Geula for bringing these aspects of the illuminations on 8v and 20v to my attention and sharing his observations and research about the Hasidei Ashkenaz. If our analysis of the artistic production is correct and Asher ben Isaac was the artist as well as scribe of this manuscript, it suggests that he was aware of this custom.

33. Fols 8v and 89r. The hand held to the cheek with a tilted head is a gesture of mourning in Christian art of the medieval period; see for example: D.C. Shorr, 'The Mourning Virgin and St. John', *The Art Bulletin* 22:2 (1940), figs 7, 9, 12, 15, 16. I am grateful to Dr. Karl-Georg Pfändtner for bringing this to my attention and his help with issues concerning the iconography of MS. Opp. 776.

34. For a more detailed discussion see A. Geula, *Lost Aggadic Works Known Only from Ashkenaz: Midrash Abkir, Midrash Esfa and Devarim Zuta* (in Hebrew), Ph.D. thesis, Hebrew University of Jerusalem, 2006, 308–13.

35. 'Visual culture' here referring to a limited and specific milieu, as used by J.F. Hamburger in his book *Nuns as Artists: The Visual Culture of a Medieval Convent* (Berkeley, 1997).

36. For further documentary evidence and discussion of Jewish musical activity during the late Middle Ages and early Renaissance, see K. Moens, 'De eerste violisten in Antwerpen: 1554–1560', *Musica antiqua: Actuele informatie over oude muziek* 11/4 (1994), 170–73; see further works noted above by Salmen.

37. סליק. ב'נ'ל'ך .(ברוך נותן ליעף כוח)

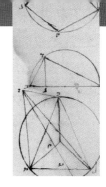

CHAPTER 7

Science as a Meeting-place of Cultures: The Court of Emperor Frederick II and Judah ben Solomon ha-Kohen's Midrash ha-Hokhmah

Sabine Arndt

Frederick II (1194–1250), Holy Roman Emperor of the Staufen dynasty, is one of the most famous and controversial emperors of the Middle Ages. His reign was marked by a constant struggle for power with the papacy, resulting in two excommunications, but it was at his court that the arts and sciences were cultivated and flourished.

Raised in Sicily, which at that time was a melting pot of Latin, Arabic, Greek and Hebrew cultures, Frederick is said to have spoken no fewer than six languages: apart from the common language of Sicily and Apulia (*volgare*), which was his native language, he knew Latin, German, French, and perhaps even some Greek and Arabic. He was very interested in the arts, philosophy and the natural sciences, engaged in numerous building projects, founded the University of Naples, commissioned translations of scientific texts from Arabic into Latin, invited scientists to his court and engaged in discussions with them. He even wrote a scientific work of his own: *De arte venandi cum avibus* (On the art of hunting with birds) is a treatise on birds and falconry that remained a standard work on the subject up until modern times. His unquenchable thirst for knowledge is legendary – already in his own time he was known as *stupor mundi*, amazement of the world. Particularly striking is the way he had letters containing lists of philosophic and scientific questions sent to renowned scientists all over the world. Christian, Muslim and Jewish philosophers report of letters they received from the emperor, containing questions on subjects that ranged from geology to metaphysics. The imperial court, in the person of the emperor himself, was a meeting-place of culture.[1]

Leonardo of Pisa, also known as Fibonacci (*c.* 1170–after 1240), who had studied Arabic mathematics in North Africa and Syria, is just one example. He had been invited to the court where he engaged in mathematical discussions with the emperor in the presence of the philosophers.[2] He even dedicated a work, *Liber quadratorum*, to the emperor. The revised version of his major work, *Liber abaci*, was dedicated to one of Frederick's philosophers, Michael Scot (*c.* 1175–*c.* 1235).

This physician, alchemist and astrologer of Scottish origin was certainly the first person Frederick would turn to with his questions.[3] Before joining the court of the emperor, he had spent several years in Toledo, where he had translated different scientific books from Arabic into Latin. In Italy Michael worked as Frederick's court astrologer, continued translating and composed scientific works of his own. In his *Liber introductorius*, an encyclopaedic work in three major parts, Michael mentions numerous questions that were posed to him by the emperor; he gives a list of some fifty queries. The topics range from hydrology and volcanology to the whereabouts of the hereafter and God's residence. Michael answers most of them, not without praising the emperor for his great learning.[4]

But Frederick did not restrict his search to Christian Europe. A list of questions on philosophy, geometry and mathematics was sent to the Ayyubid sultan Al-Kamil (1180–1238) in Egypt, who forwarded them to his sages.[5] Another set of questions was sent to the mathematician Kamal al-Din Ibn Yunus (d. *c.* 1285) in Mosul (Iraq).[6] But the most famous questions answered by Muslim scholars are probably the 'Sicilian questions' on Aristotelian philosophy that were sent to the North African philosopher Ibn Sab'in.[7]

Although the authenticity of some of these reports has been questioned recently, and some of the questions actually stem from older works,[8] the mass of different sources makes it clear that the emperor had a habit of sending questions to scientists of both Christian and Muslim descent. Unclear, however, remain Frederick's motives for doing so. It almost seems as if the emperor was using the scientific community as a search engine. Whenever he had any kind of question, he just sent an enquiry; somewhere in the world wide web of the day there had to be an answer.

Jews were not excluded from the emperor's search for knowledge and wisdom. One of his enquiries reached the Jewish scholar Judah ben Solomon ha-Kohen (b. *c.* 1215), author of the encyclopaedic work *Midrash ha-Hokhmah* (Explanation of science).[9] Judah was born in Toledo, which had been under Arab rule from the eighth to the eleventh century. In Judah's time its population still consisted of a mix of Mozarabs, or 'Arabized' Christians, Muslims and Jews. Arabic remained the language of culture and religion for a large part of the population. It is therefore not surprising that Judah composed his

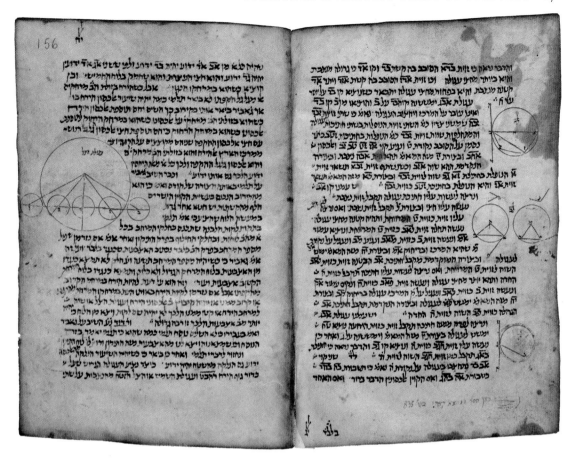

Midrash ha-Hokhmah in Arabic. The encyclopaedic work comprises abbreviations and summaries of the most important scientific books of the time. Unfortunately, the Arabic original of the work is no longer extant. In his Hebrew translation Judah reports that at the age of 18 he received a letter written in Arabic by the 'philosopher of the emperor', who asked him several questions. He answered the philosopher, adding questions of his own, which initiated a whole correspondence. About ten years later he travelled to Italy to visit the emperor's court. There (in the years 1245–47) he translated the *Midrash ha-Hokhmah* into the Hebrew language. It is considered the oldest extant Hebrew encyclopaedia of science and philosophy and one of the earliest sources that made secular sciences available to a Jewish readership that did not speak Arabic (figure 56). The work covers Aristotelian logic, natural philosophy and metaphysics, Euclidian geometry, astronomy, cosmology and astrology. In addition, it contains three treatises dedicated to traditional Jewish learning (the explanation of biblical verses, the letters of the Hebrew alphabet and Talmudic aggadot).[10] This combination of secular science and religious teaching might be surprising, but it reflects Judah's twofold

Figure 56
Judah ben Solomon ha-Kohen's *Midrash ha-Hokhmah. right* Hebrew translation of Euclid's *Elements* III.31–33 (32–34 in the Greek edition). *left* Hebrew translation of *Almagest* VI.7, on the computation of the duration of solar and lunar eclipses. Several quires are missing between the two pages (Byzantium, *c.* 1300). Oxford, Bodleian Library, MS. Mich. 551, fols 155v–156r.

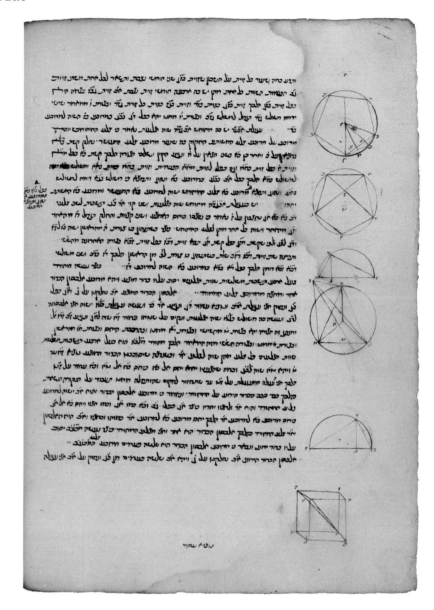

aim in compiling the encyclopaedia. On the one hand, he tried to convince the Jews of the benefits of the secular sciences. In his view the Jews' ignorance of the sciences would cause the nations, who prided themselves on their scientific works, to look down upon the Jews. On the other hand, Judah tried to cause those who erred and wasted their time studying these sciences to return to the Torah.[11] In other words, he wanted his co-religionists to avail themselves of the latest scholarly products of the surrounding non-Jewish society.

That Judah himself was an important member of the scientific community can clearly be seen from the discussion he had with the philosopher of the emperor. The identity of this philosopher

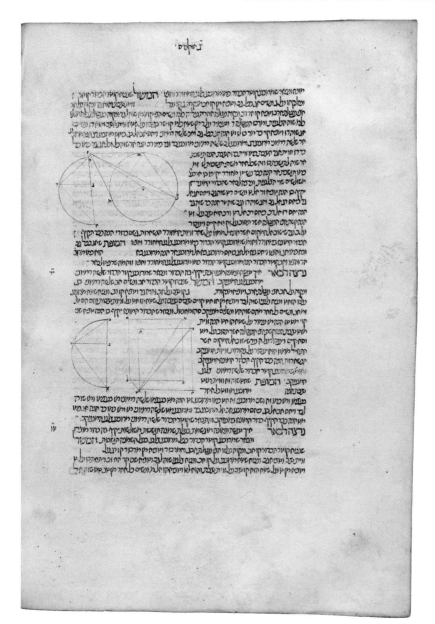

Figure 58
Moses Ibn Tibbon's
Hebrew translation
of Euclid's *Elements*
XIII (construction of a
tetrahedron and a cube),
completed in 1270 (Spain,
fifteenth century). Oxford,
Bodleian Library, MS.
Hunt. 16, fol. 83v.

remains uncertain,[12] and Judah does not supply much information about the circumstances in which the correspondence took place. He is apparently more interested in reporting the discussion of two specific topics. First, he conveys the philosopher's question:[13] 'How do we construct each of the five platonic solids on a given sphere? And how do we construct the given sphere inside each of them?' This question relates to the thirteenth book of Euclid's *Elements*, in which Euclid shows how to construct each of the five platonic solids (tetrahedron, cube, octahedron, dodecahedron and icosahedron) and to circumscribe spheres on them (figures 57 and 58).[14] The philosopher,

אחר המחבר

אמן

Figure 59 *pp. 90–1*
Midrash ha-Hokhmah:
Judah ha-Kohen's
refutation of the
philosopher (Byzantium,
mid-fifteenth century).
Oxford, Bodleian Library,
MS. Mich. 400, fol.
36v–37r.

Figure 60 *right*
Sefer Mileus: Jacob
ben Makhir's Hebrew
translation of Menelaus'
Sphaerics (completed
in 1271), prop. I. 16–17
(Spain, fifteenth century).
Oxford, Bodleian Library,
MS. Hunt. 16, fol. 111r.

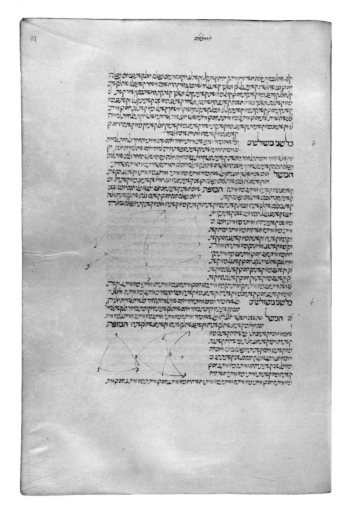

however, wants to know how to do the opposite, namely how to inscribe spheres within the solids. Well-versed in Euclidean geometry, Judah answers this question without difficulty. At the end of his response he writes (figure 59):

> This is what I managed to answer the philosopher of the emperor when I was 18 years old. I also asked several questions myself, and what I am going to write now is one of them. It was to give a clear geometric proof for the tables of ascensions in the oblique sphere. The one who is called 'philosopher' answered me at that time in Arabic as follows. I have translated it into Hebrew …

The question that Judah asks the philosopher relates to astronomy. He refers to tables of *oblique ascension*: they calculate arcs of the celestial equator that rise with arcs of the ecliptic depending on the

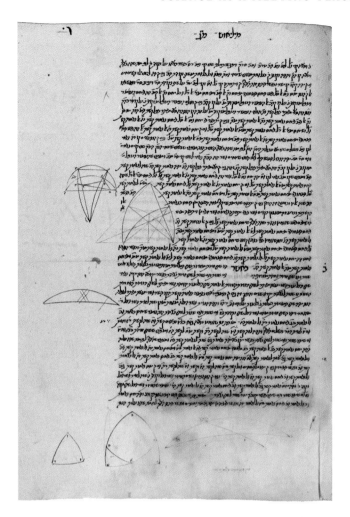

Figure 61
Sefer Mileus: Jacob
ben Makhir's Hebrew
translation of Menelaus'
Sphaerics, prop. III.1
(known as 'Menelaus'
theorem') and III.2
(Constantinople (Turkey),
1507). Oxford, Bodleian
Library, MS. Hunt. 96,
fol. 36r.

position of the observer on the earth.[15] Knowing which part of the
equator was rising at the same time as a certain part of the ecliptic
was important for timekeeping as well as astrology. Tables containing these data had already been made in antiquity by the famous
astronomer Ptolemy (second century CE). They had continuously
been revised and improved by scientists in Islamic countries, who
introduced Indian and Iranian methods of calculation into Greek
astronomy. Many of these tables were distributed in astronomical
handbooks, called *zij* in Arabic. *Zijes* contained different kinds of data
tables needed for the calculation of the positions of the stars and the
planets, but they also covered other topics such as timekeeping and
astrological computations. These compilations were quite popular in
the Arab world. Over 200 different *zijes* were produced between the
eighth and the fifteenth centuries. At the time of the correspondence,
the 1230s, only a few *zijes* were available in Latin, the most famous
being the Toledan Tables.[16]

In his answer the philosopher uses spherical geometry in order to find the so-called equation of daylight, or ascensional difference, which is the difference between the rising time of a certain part of the ecliptic as seen from the terrestrial equator and its rising time as seen from any other point in the northern hemisphere. Judah presents the philosopher's explanation and then writes:[17]

> I gave him several answers to this explanation and to the diagram he had made, constructed on the last page.[18] I answered him regarding this matter: On [error] and on errors that are not appropriate for a student who is called 'philosopher' like you ...

What follows is a mocking, even sarcastic, refutation of the philosopher. Judah's critique is based on one major point. First, the philosopher had claimed that two particular spherical triangles are *similar* – that is, that they contain the same angles respectively. Then he had claimed that those triangles have different sizes. In spherical geometry, however, that is impossible. There is no such thing as *similar* triangles on one given sphere: if two triangles on the same sphere contain the same angles, then the triangles are *equal*. In other words, the philosopher had confused plane and spherical geometry. This explains Judah's sarcasm: his colleague had made such a fundamental mistake that he did not deserve to be called 'philosopher'. If he truly believed that the same rules applied to spherical and plane triangles, Judah concludes, 'he has to help us with this novelty that has come about under the sun'. Of course, this request for help is ironic, for it is well known that 'there is nothing new under the sun' (Eccl. 1:9).

Judah's refutation of the philosopher was furthermore based on propositions I.17 (figure 60) and III.2 (figure 61) of the *Sphaerics* by the Greek mathematician Menelaus of Alexandria (around 100 CE).[19] This 'Book of Menelaus' is a basic work on spherical geometry.[20] Together with other works on theoretical astronomy, such as *The Rotating Sphere* by Autolycus (fourth century BCE) and the *Sphaerics* by Theodosius (second century BCE), it was considered in the Arabic-speaking world as belonging to the 'intermediary writings', namely intermediary between the study of Euclid's *Elements* and Ptolemy's *Almagest*. These books contained the mathematics that a reader needed in order to understand the *Almagest*, or 'astronomy proper'.[21] Obviously Judah's colleague had either not read or not understood a basic work on theoretical astronomy, a work one was supposed to read before studying the *Almagest*, and that Judah himself had mastered at the age of 18. Furthermore, the problem the philosopher is trying to solve is by no means a difficult one: it had already been solved in Ptolemy's *Almagest* and, using different methods, by generations of Arab astronomers after him. How, then, could the Philosopher of the Holy Roman Emperor make such a major mistake?

The historicity of Judah's account is open to question. Of course, the story of the philosopher's mistake serves several purposes. On the one hand, it is a demonstration of Judah's great learning – at the age of 18 he was able to vanquish the emperor's philosopher in argument. There may also be a polemical dimension to this story. As stated above, one of Judah's goals in writing a scientific encyclopaedia was to demonstrate that the Jews were equal to the nations in their mastery of the sciences. This goal Judah himself had certainly achieved: an emperor's philosopher, a representative of the wisdom of the nations, had been beaten at his own game, the sciences, by a Jew. After Judah's refutation, this representative could certainly not pride himself on 'his' sciences any more.

In addition, Judah shows how his great learning and therefore his triumph were achieved. In his answer to the question on platonic solids he had already demonstrated that he had mastered the standard work on plane geometry, Euclid's *Elements*. In his refutation of the philosopher he explicitly mentions a conditional syllogism, a statement of the form 'If A, then B'. He had therefore clearly been educated in logic. Finally, he shows that he has also mastered Menelaus' *Sphaerics*, one of the 'intermediary writings'. But logic, Euclidian geometry and the *Sphaerics*, in that order, constitute the scientific curriculum Judah had recommended at the beginning of the *Midrash ha-Hokhmah*.[22] It would appear that Judah wishes to tell his readers not only about his own triumph. In proving that at a young age he had been able to demonstrate that Jews are equal, if not superior to the gentiles in scientific learning he exhorts his readers to study the books recommended by him (or, for that matter, the *Midrash ha-Hokhmah*) in order to achieve what he had achieved.

There is one strong argument in favour of the authenticity of this account. Judah made the Hebrew translation of the *Midrash ha-Hokhmah* in Italy, from where he may have been in contact with the court. The risk of detection would have been far too great for him to invent such a story. Although it is highly improbable that either the philosopher or the emperor could read Hebrew, they would have eventually been informed about Judah's account of the philosopher's mistake.

There are two possible explanations as to why the philosopher made the mistake. Either Judah is right in assuming that for some reason he simply didn't know better, or the philosopher knowingly made the mistake. If the latter is the case, the correspondence between Judah and the philosopher gains a new perspective. Instead of asking and answering questions out of scientific interest the philosopher might actually have been testing his opponent,[23] and was deliberately giving a wrong answer in order see whether the young man from Toledo was able to spot the mistake. With his refutation Judah would certainly have 'passed the test' and thus have shown that he was worthy of the philosopher's and therefore the emperor's attention.

On the other hand, it is for several reasons quite conceivable that the philosopher was not aware of the mistake he was making. Whereas in the Arab world the study and practice of Greek astronomy had been established for centuries, the Latin West had at the time of the correspondence only just begun to discover its benefits. It was due to translations from the Arabic that the works of famous Greek and Arab astronomers began to be known in the West. This translation movement had started in the twelfth century; its centre was Judah's home town, Toledo.[24] Of course, this does not mean that the philosopher himself did not have access to any astronomical writings. Since he knew Arabic he could have read the relevant books in the original. The fundamental mistake he made, however, shows that he was not familiar with basic spherical trigonometry. A possible explanation is that he had gained his astronomical knowledge not from theoretical works but from sets of astronomical tables or *zijes*. As they contained all the relevant data and instructions on how to calculate with them, an astronomer did not necessarily need to know all the underlying theories in order to use them. In other words, the philosopher might have had the relevant data and could work with them, but he did not know how they were derived. Judah, on the other hand, did have the mathematical training that was necessary to understand the trigonometry behind the data. But if he understood the theoretical part, did he already know the answer to his question when he asked it? Is Judah's question therefore a test? It may of course be a part of scientific polemics. But, as stated above, this problem would not have been difficult to solve for an Arab mathematician. Curiously, Judah does not choose to tell the philosopher the correct solution to the problem, which can also be found in Menelaus' *Sphaerics*.[25] This might be explained by the fact that Menelaus' work deals with trigonometry proper and not with astronomy; astronomical implementations of the theorems are not mentioned. Judah has obviously finished the theoretical part of his training when he answers the philosopher, but he may not have yet started to study books on astronomy. His question therefore seems to be asked out of genuine curiosity; he knows the astronomical tables and is interested in a geometrical explanation for the data they contain.

We are informed that Judah's refutation was reported to the emperor, who was 'very pleased' with it, and that ten years later Judah visited his court, where he translated his *Midrash ha-Hokhmah* into Hebrew.[26] His decision to render a translation was certainly influenced by the fact that most of his Italian co-religionists did not know Arabic and were unable to study Greek mathematical sciences in the Arabic tradition, which had made Judah an equal even to the emperor's philosopher. Furthermore, many of these works had already been translated into Latin and were therefore available to a Christian readership. If the Jews of Italy were to be an equal part of society as regards knowledge of sciences, they needed to keep up with this development. They had to be taught Greek sciences in their own language of religion and culture. On the other hand, knowledge of the sciences should not lead to a loss of their own religious and cultural identity. By trying to achieve both goals Judah created the first encyclopaedic work that transmitted comprehensive knowledge of different branches of secular science and philosophy to the Jews in the Latin West.

The correspondence shows the truly intercultural dialogue characteristic of the court of Frederick II; it is the Hebrew translation of letters written in Arabic by a Jew in Spain and a Christian in Italy discussing Greek science advanced by Muslims. The knowledge that had made Judah triumph over the philosopher had been gained from Arabic scientific writings, while the *Midrash ha-Hokhmah*, the oldest extant Hebrew encyclopaedia of science and philosophy, made these sciences available to Judah's co-religionists in Christian Europe.

NOTES

1. On the scientific culture at the court of Frederick II, see D. Abulafia, *Frederick II: A Medieval Emperor* (London, 2002), 251–89; W. Stürner, *Friedrich II. Teil 2. Der Kaiser 1220–1250* (Darmstadt, 2000), 342–457; C.H. Haskins, *Studies in the History of Mediaeval Science* (Cambridge, Mass., 1924), 242–71; C. Sirat, 'Les traducteurs juifs a la cour des rois de Sicile et de Naples', in Geneviève Contamine, ed., *Traduction et traducteurs au Moyen Âge* (Paris, 1989), 169–91.

2. See R. Rashed, 'Fibonacci et les mathématiques arabes', *Micrologus* 2 (1994), 145–60.

3. On Michael Scot, see Haskins, *Studies*, 272–98; C. Burnett, 'Michael Scot and the Transmission of Scientific Culture from Toledo to Bologna via the Court of Frederick II Hohenstaufen, *Micrologus* 2 (1994), 101–26.

4. The list has been edited by G. Grebner, 'Der Liber Nemroth, die Fragen Friedrichs II. an Michael Scotus und die Redaktionen des Liber particularis', in G. Grebner and J. Fried, eds, *Kulturtransfer und Hofgesellschaft im Mittelalter. Wissenskultur am sizilianischen und kastilischen Hof im 13. Jahrhundert* (Berlin, 2008), 285–98.

5. See F. Gabrieli, *Die Kreuzzüge aus arabischer Sicht* (Augsburg, 1999), 329.

6. D.N. Hasse, 'Mosul and Frederick II Hohenstaufen: Notes on Atiraddin al-Abhari and Siragaddin al-Urmawi', in I. Draelants, A. Tihon and B. van den Abeele, eds, *Occident et Proche-Orient. Contacts scientifiques au temps des Croisdes* (Turnhout, 2000), 145–63.

7. An Arabic edition with German translation was made by A. A. Akasoy, *Philosophie und Mystik in der späten Almohadenzeit. Die sizilianischen Fragen des Ibn Sab'in* (Leiden, 2006).

8. See Akasoy, *Philosophie und Mystik*, 107–24; Grebner, 'Der Liber Nemroth'.

9. On Judah ben Solomon ha-Kohen and the *Midrash ha-Hokhmah*, see, for example, C. Sirat, 'Juda B. Salomon Ha-Cohen: philosophe, astronome et peut-être kabbaliste de la première moitié du XIIIe siècle', *Italia* 2 (1978), 39–61; M. Steinschneider, *Die hebräischen Übersetzungen des Mittelalters und die Juden als Dolmetscher* (Berlin 1893; repr. 1956), 1–4; S. Harvey, ed., *The Medieval Hebrew Encyclopedias of Science and Philosophy* (Dordrecht, 2000), especially the articles by R. Fontaine, Y.T. Langermann and T. Lévy. The volume also contains an English translation of the relevant passage of Steinschneider, *Hebräische Übersetzungen*.

10. For a more detailed overview of the contents, see R. Fontaine, 'Judah ben Solomon ha-Cohen's "Midrash ha-Hokhmah": Its Sources and Use of Sources', in *Medieval Hebrew Encyclopedias*, 191–210.

11. Oxford, Bodleian Library, MS. Mich. 551, fol. 45v; see also Fontaine, 'Judah ben Solomon ha-Cohen's "Midrash ha-Hokhmah"', 202.

12. Possible candidates are Michael Scot, John of Palermo and Theodore of Antioch. All of them belonged to Frederick's court and stood, for example, in contact with Fibonacci. See: Haskins, *Studies*, 242–98; Stürner, *Friedrich II*, 342–57; C. Burnett, 'Master Theodore, Frederick II's Philosopher', in *Federico II e le nuove culture. Atti del XXXI Convegno storico internazionale* (Spoleto, 1995), 225–85.

13. The correspondence is translated from MS. Mich. 400, fols 35r–37r.

14. *Elements*, XIII.13–17.

15. A short introduction to medieval mathematical astronomy can be found in G. van Brummelen, *The Mathematics of the Heavens and the Earth: The Early History of Trigonometry* (Princeton and Oxford, 2009), 1–8. On ascensions see D.A. King, 'al-Matali'', *Encyclopedia of Islam*, vol. VI. (Leiden, 1991), 792–4.

16. See E.S. Kennedy, 'A Survey of Islamic Astronomical Tables', *Transactions of the American Philosophical Society* 46:2 (1956), 123–77; the work has been updated by D.A. King, J. Samsó and B.R. Goldstein, 'Astronomical Handbooks and Tables from the Islamic World (750–1900): An Interim Report', *Suhayl* 2 (2001), 9–105.

17. MS. Mich. 400, fol. 37r (figure 59).

18. Unfortunately, the philosopher's diagram was not transmitted in the *Midrash ha-Hokhmah*.

19. An Arabic edition and German translation of the *Sphaerics* were rendered by M. Krause, *Die Sphärik von Menelaos aus Alexandrien in der Verbesserung von Abu Nasr Mansur b. Ali Ibn Iraq* (Berlin, 1936).

20. On Menelaus' *Sphaerics* and its influence on Arab astronomy, see G. van Brummelen, *Mathematics of the Heavens and the Earth*, 53–63 and 173–85.

21. See T. Lévy, 'The Establishment of the Mathematical Bookshelf of the Medieval Hebrew Scholar (XIIIth–XIVth century): Translations and Translators', *Science in Context* 10:3 (1997), 431–51 at 444–6.

22. T. Lévy, 'Mathematics in the "Midrash ha-Hokhmah" of Judah ben Solomon ha-Cohen', in *Medieval Hebrew Encyclopedias*, 300.

23. In fact, the same conclusion was drawn by several Arabic chroniclers regarding questions the emperor had sent to Muslim scholars. See Akasoy, *Philosophie und Mystik*, 111.

24. On Toledo as the centre of the translation movement, see C. Burnett, 'The Coherence of the Arabic–Latin Translation Program in Toledo in the Twelfth Century', *Science in Context* 14 (2001), 249–88.

25. The philosopher had erroneously tried to apply prop. III.2, which later became known as the 'Rule of four quantities'. The problem he discussed could have been solved by use of prop. III.3, the 'Law of the tangents'.

26. MS. Mich. 400, fol. 37r.

CHAPTER 8

Jews and Christians Imagining the Temple

Lesley Smith

The Temple in Jerusalem – God's dwelling on earth – was a potent image for medieval Jews. There had been, in fact, more than one building. According to the biblical book of Kings (1 Kings, chapters 5–8), the first Temple was built on Mount Moriah in the reign of Solomon (c. 970–c. 930 BCE), and served as the centre of worship in Israel; only here could the sacrifice of animals be made, on the altar of the holocaust. This original Temple survived for about four hundred years, but was destroyed by the Babylonians when the Israelites were taken into exile, around 586 BCE. The Prophet Ezekiel provided visionary descriptions of a second Temple (Ezekiel, chapters 40–48), which was constructed when the Jews returned from their captivity in Babylon, around 520 BCE. It too was eventually desecrated by Antiochus IV Epiphanes in 167 BCE. Re-dedicated by Judas Maccabeus and restored by Herod the Great, this second Temple was the building standing at the time of Jesus, and was the scene of some of the events of his life. This Temple was razed and looted by the Romans in 70 CE, an event commemorated in relief sculptures on the Arch of Titus in Rome (figure 62).

Yet Jews held out hope for the restoration of the Temple in the coming messianic age. For this reason, written descriptions of the Temple complex of buildings were studied with particular care, since they described the house of God as it had been and as it would be again. The holiest part of the Temple was patterned on the Tabernacle, the earlier (and originally portable) structure, which housed the Ark of the Covenant and was the focus of sacrificial worship (Exodus, chapters 25–31; 35–40). Its outer courtyard housed the menorah (the seven-branched lamp stand) and the table with the showbread (twelve loaves of unleavened bread, offered to God, representing the twelve tribes of Israel). The unparalleled importance of both the Tabernacle

and the Temple, as places where God had promised to be present
on earth, is reflected in the appearance of Temple furnishings in
extant synagogue floor mosaics from the fourth century CE onwards.
From the tenth century, similar images of Tabernacle and Temple
implements can be found in full-page (or double-page) illustrations
in Hebrew Bibles.

One such 'carpet' page can be found in an early-fourteenth-century
Bible in the Bodleian collections, originally from Castile, although
the page itself appears to be a slightly later addition (MS. Canon. Or.

94, fol. 1r, figure 63). Central to the once-gilded illustration is the menorah. To the right are two musical instruments named as trumpets, a covered round laver or bowl, and two flesh hooks which would have been used in the burning of sacrificial offerings. The objects on the left have been damaged, but include spoons and another bowl.

Pages like this are not intended to be primarily decorative, in the way that patterned borders or text frames, for example, decorate

Figure 63
Hebrew Bible (Castile, early fourteenth century). Oxford, Bodleian Library, MS. Canon. Or. 94, fol. 1r.

some Christian manuscripts. Rather, they are a supplementary aid to understanding important features of the biblical text, and a means of impressing on the reader's memory visually the furnishings of the place where God resides.

Some medieval Jewish scholars continued and extended this use of illustration in their own interpretation of religious texts. Rabbi Solomon ben Isaac (1040–1105), known as Rashi, working in Troyes in northern France, was one such. In a letter to the rabbis of nearby Auxerre, in answer to a query from one of them about his commentary on Ezekiel's vision, Rashi writes:

> [W]ith regard to what he [one of the Auxerre rabbis] wrote … concerning the northern outer chambers, about not being able to understand where they began to the north-west and how much they extended to the east… I cannot add anything to what I explained in my commentary, but I shall draw a plan of them and send it to him.

The plan Rashi mentions can be identified with the second of the two diagrams which, together with two maps (for Numbers, chapter 34), are found in most copies of Rashi's commentaries, almost always identical in form. From the evidence of the letter, it seems very probable that these images were produced by Rashi himself as part of his exposition of the text. The Bodleian copy of Rashi on the Prophets includes both diagrams in the book of Ezekiel. Written in France *c.* 1300, the manuscript uses a display script for the biblical text in the inner column (or columns) of each page, and outside it Rashi's commentary in a less formal handwriting. This handsome volume is written with a strong awareness of the layout of the page. The shape and size of the manuscript, and the regularity of the script, make it strongly reminiscent of a Torah scroll; and yet the differentiation of biblical text and commentary text, each complete but separate from the other, also suggests that the layout has been influenced by some types of medieval Christian Bible commentary. The page illustrated in figure 64 (MS. Opp. 2, fol. 207r) includes Rashi's diagram of the division of the Promised Land, from his commentary on the Prophet Ezekiel. It shows the disposition of the twelve tribes, as well as the priests and levites, with the sanctuary of the Temple at their heart (figure 65).

A second set of drawings, this time in Rashi's Exodus commentary and illustrating the Tabernacle furnishings, show more variation and are not present in all the early copies of his work; so scholars are not

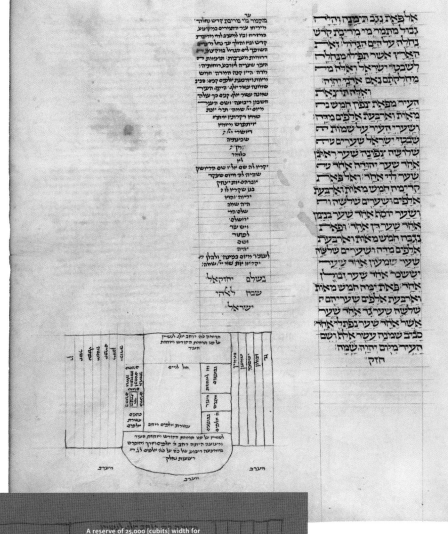

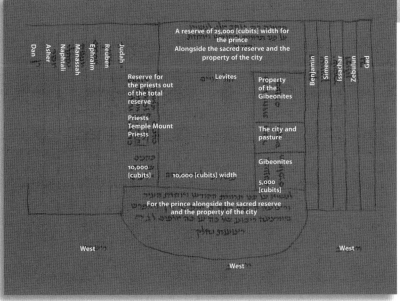

Figure 64
Rashi's diagram of
the division of
the Promised Land from his
commentary on Ezekiel
48 (France (?), *c.* 1300).
Oxford, Bodleian Library,
MS. Opp. 2, fol. 207r.

Figure 65
Rashi's diagram of the
division of the Promised
Land (in English
translation).
Oxford, Bodleian Library,
MS. Opp. 2, fol. 207r.

Figure 66
Rashi's commentary on
Exodus 25 (France, early
thirteenth century).
Oxford, Bodleian Library,
MS. Opp. Add. fol. 69,
fol. 40r.

quite so sure that they originate with Rashi himself. Nevertheless, as
with the maps and diagrams, some of these drawings are located *within*
the text, physically integrated with the commentary, rather than being
simply additions in the margins. One such can be seen in a Bodleian
manuscript of Rashi's commentary on the Five Books of Moses, here
showing an illustration of the menorah (figure 66, MS. Opp. Add. fol.
69, fol. 40r). This placement suggests a rather greater likelihood that the
drawings were an original part of the commentary, and of their being
conceptually as well as physically part of Rashi's interpretation.

One of Rashi's characteristics as a scriptural commentator is his
interest in *peshat*, which we might translate as the literal or plain
meaning of a text. Rather than concentrating on the midrashic interpretations of the Bible, Rashi begins as far as possible with a literal
reading. He considers the detail of the biblical text, attempting to
reconcile apparent differences, and to show how the text could be
concretely understood. Referring as he does to rabbinic non-literal
tradition in his exegesis of the text, Rashi focuses on its plain meaning
by invoking the Targum, the Aramaic paraphrase, and 'leazim', the
French vernacular renderings of Hebrew words.

From about the middle of the twelfth century, some Christian
commentators also began to take a new interest in the literal meaning
of the Bible. Paris was the centre of Christian biblical study in the
Middle Ages, and one school, that of the Order of Augustinian
Canons at the abbey of St Victor, looked anew at the literal sense
of the biblical text. The head of the school, Hugh, and two of his
scholarly successors, Richard and Andrew, were at the forefront of
this movement. Hugh of St Victor (d. 1142) was a renowned biblical
scholar who believed that any valid interpretation of the scriptural
text had to begin squarely with the literal meaning. He likened understanding the Bible to constructing a building: one had to begin with
the foundations of the literal sense, before one could move on to the
structure itself (allegory) and its decoration (moral interpretations);
and 'just as you see that every building lacking a foundation cannot
stand firm, so it is with learning' (Hugh of St Victor, *Didascalicon*,
book 6). In order better to understand the literal meaning, these
Victorines sought out Jewish scholars who could explain readings of
the Hebrew Bible. They probably did not learn any Hebrew themselves
(although occasional Christian scholars such as Herbert of Bosham
did – see the essay by De Visscher in this volume), but it would
have been perfectly possible for them to discuss these questions with
Jewish scholars in the vernacular: Rashi himself lectured in French.

Although Richard of St Victor (d. 1173) was best known for his
writings on the spiritual life, he too was firmly grounded in the

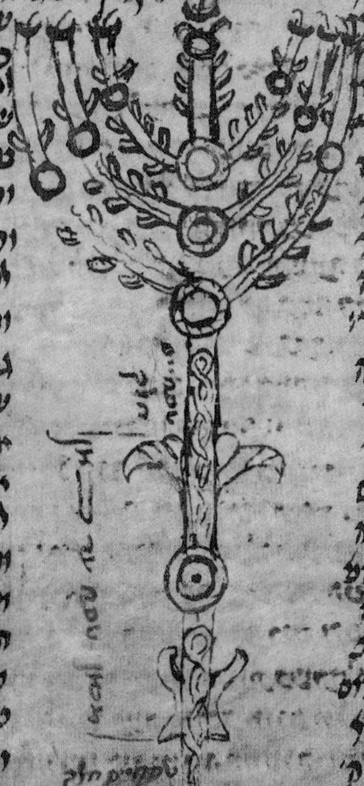

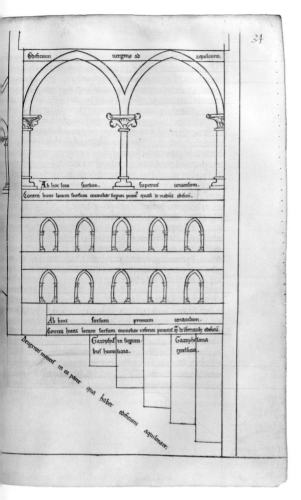

knowledge of Scripture. His works of biblical exegesis include an exposition of Ezekiel's prophetic vision of the Temple. From its beginning, Richard's text came with a set of diagrams, which were integral to his analysis. Thirteen plans and elevations of the building are customarily found embedded within the commentary, presenting visually and clarifying Richard's understanding of Ezekiel's text, and his fascination with problems such as how to build on the side of a hill: more than one of the diagrams picture how this might have been done (figure 67, MS. Bodl. 459, fol. 34r). A few manuscripts add a fourteenth diagram at the end of the text (figure 68, MS. Bodl. 459, fol. 37v). If we compare it to Rashi's diagram of the disposition of the tribes in the Promised Land (figure 64), the similarities are obvious – seven tribes lined up on the left, and five on the right; the priest and levites between them; and the sanctuary of the Temple in the midst of them all. It is not far-fetched to imagine that Richard saw manuscripts of Rashi's Ezekiel commentary, and copied the diagram for inclusion in his own work. The abbey of St Victor had an excellent library of its own, and Paris was a meeting point for scholars from all over Europe (some of whom, we know, deposited their own

Figure 67
Richard of St Victor: building on a hill (England, early thirteenth century). Oxford, Bodleian Library, MS. Bodl. 459, fol. 34r.

books in the St Victor library for safekeeping). Indeed, Richard's confrère and contemporary, Andrew (d. 1175), was so interested in Jewish interpretations that he was accused by some Christian scholars of 'judaising' – in effect, going native, and becoming more Jewish than the Jews. As well as citing more traditional Jewish exposition, Andrew reports explanations of texts given to him by contemporary scholars, and in a number of cases prefers the Jewish interpretation over accepted Christian teaching.

The Victorine scholars were too early to know the work of Rabbi Moses ben Maimon, known as Maimonides (1137/8–1204), but he became familiar to other late-twelfth- and thirteenth-century Christian theologians. Maimonides worked originally in Cordoba, but later moved to Fustat (Old Cairo), where a number of manuscripts he owned of his own works (in some cases, written in his own hand) were preserved. One of these works is his commentary on the Mishnah, the most important early collection of Jewish oral law, which includes sections on the Temple and its practices. Like Rashi, Maimonides occasionally used diagrams as an aid to his textual exposition. Figure 69 (MS. Poc. 295, fol. 295r) shows the Bodleian copy of parts four and five of his Mishnah commentary. This late-twelfth-century manuscript was Maimonides' own copy (it belonged to his family for several generations), and is thought to have been written by the rabbi himself. It contains ten drawings depicting the layout and furniture of the Temple, including this floorplan, with its clear placing of the altar for burning sacrifices, and the menorah.

One medieval expositor was particularly influential in introducing Jewish scholarship to his fellow Christian theologians. Nicholas of Lyra (d. 1349) was a Franciscan, working in Paris, who wrote a massive commentary on the entire Bible (the *Postilla in totam bibliam*), which became a ubiquitous text. Nicholas was intensely interested in the literal meaning of the Bible as being the only firm foundation for correct belief, and this led him to look to Jewish sources for closer readings of the original texts. Nicholas probably knew some Hebrew; certainly he knew the contents of Hebrew texts, especially (but not exclusively) those by Rashi. Rashi is mentioned by name in Nicholas's Prologue to the *Postilla*: 'I intend', he says, 'not only to use the words of the Catholic Doctors, but also those of the Hebrews, especially Rabbi Solomon among the Hebrew doctors, who is better at interpreting the literal sense.' Whilst he never strays from Christian orthodoxy, Nicholas shows an enormous admiration – and preference – for the Jewish readings of the text; so much so that his work is littered with phrases such as, 'the Hebrews say, and it seems correctly...', or 'the Hebrews seem to understand this better when they say...'

Nicholas also follows Rashi in using illustration to clarify his biblical interpretation. Manuscripts and early printed copies of the *Postilla* have a relatively fixed set of about thirty-five drawings, especially concentrated on illustrating those scriptural passages describing the

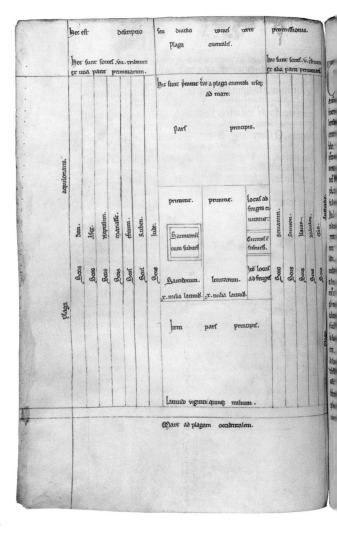

Figure 68
Richard of St Victor's diagram of the division of the Promised Land (England, early thirteenth century). Oxford, Bodleian Library, MS. Bodl. 459, fol. 37v.

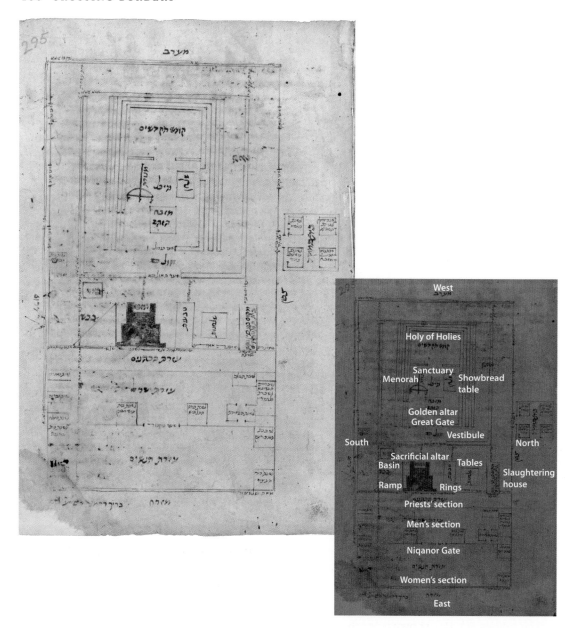

Figure 69

Maimonides, *Commentary on the Mishnah,* plan of the Temple (autograph, Fostat, *c.* 1167/8). Oxford, Bodleian Library, MS. Poc. 295, fol. 295r.

Tabernacle and the Temple (mostly in Exodus, Numbers, Kings and Ezekiel). Like Rashi, Nicholas is not concerned with simple illustration. He ignores drama, such as the crossing of the Red Sea or David killing Goliath, or moments of heightened Christian theology, such as the Crucifixion, although these are scenes often depicted in medieval Bibles and elsewhere. Showing 'what happened' is not what interests him; instead, he employs illustration as a means of making more clear his written exposition of difficult scriptural passages, especially those describing the places where God promises to be present. Often, these are open to more than one interpretation, and this is the reason why,

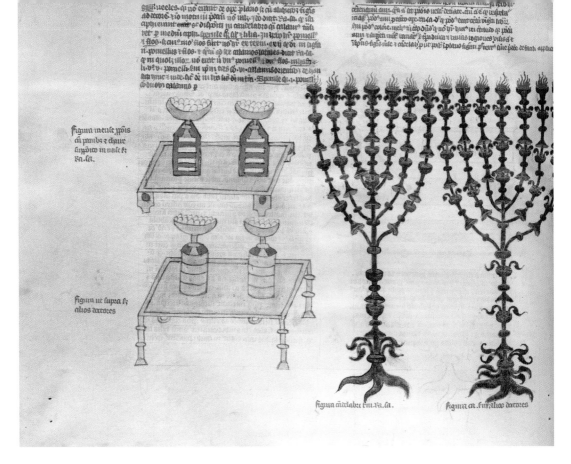

for about a third of the drawings, there is not merely one illustration but two: one showing the Christian reading and the other the Jewish – usually the reading given by Rashi.

We can see this in figure 70, which shows Nicholas's commentary on the book of Exodus, chapter 25 (MS. Bodl. 251, fol. 49v). Alongside Nicholas's text are two pairs of diagrams which illustrate the table with the showbread and the menorah. 'Cues' for each set of drawings are given in the text: 'a diagram follows'; this is true of most of the illustrations in Nicholas's commentary, and confirms that it was he who planned them and their placement in the text. Close by each drawing is a note explaining *whose* interpretation it shows: by the table with the showbread, the upper caption reads 'diagram of the table with showbread supporting the incense bowl, according to Rabbi Solomon'; the lower caption has 'the same diagram according to other learned men'. Similar phrases can be seen under the menorahs. Each of the double diagrams has a similar caption, though the formula can differ: Nicholas refers to 'Rabbi Solomon', 'learned Hebrews', 'learned Christians', 'Catholic teachers', and 'the Latins', as well as once noting the opinions of Josephus and Peter Comestor, two authoritative scholars. We should note in passing that Nicholas, in common with other Christians who used Jewish scholarly sources, will usually refer to them as 'Hebrews [*hebraei*]',

Figure 70

Nicholas of Lyra, *Commentary on Exodus*, with comparative diagrams of the menorah and the table of showbread (France, late fourteenth century). Oxford, Bodleian Library, MS. Bodl. 251, fol. 49v.

Exodi ca° xxvº.   Ibidm·

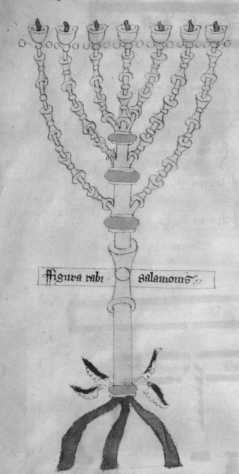

ffigura rabi   salamonis·   ffigura aliorum··

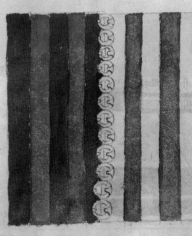

pimentu
cortinus·

pime
de fas

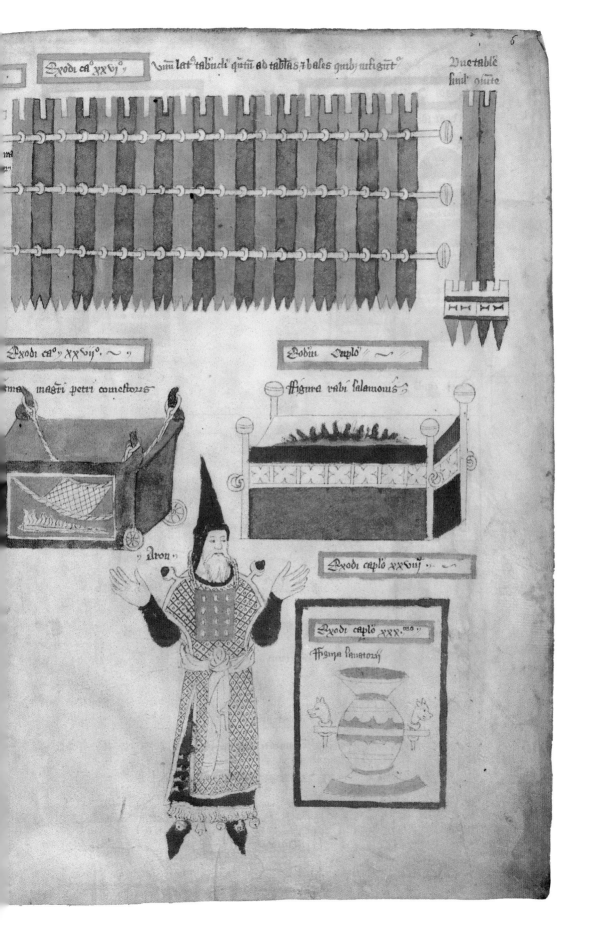

Exodi ca° xxvj°   Vin̄ lat̄ tabucl quin̄ ad tablas 7 bales qbz utisūt   Duc tabl̄ simul' giūte

Exodi ca°y xxvij° · ~ ,   Eodin̄ caplō ~

figura magri petri comectons   figura rabi salamonis

Aron

Exodi caplō xxvij ·

Exodi caplō xxx.^{mo} ·

figura lauatorij

Figure 71 *pp. 110–11*
Illustrations to Nicholas
of Lyra's *Postilla*,
including the menorah
and the High Priest
(England, *c.* 1430–40).
Oxford, Bodleian Library,
MS. Laud Misc. 156, fols
5v–6r.

Figure 72 *right*
Nicholas of Lyra,
Commentary on Ezekiel:
Temple diagram (Paris, *c.*
1500). Oxford, Bodleian
Library, MS. Canon. Bibl.
Lat. 70, fol. 165v.

rather than 'Jews [*judaei*]', since the latter term had acquired a pejorative tone in Christian usage.

Generally, the differences Nicholas is pointing out are not great; indeed, how could they be, since scholars were trying to picture the same written description? In the case of the menorah, for instance, it is a matter of decorative details, mostly on the base and shaft of the candelabrum. Sometimes Jewish scholars themselves disagreed, as Nicholas notes (on Ezekiel chapter 40): 'Not only do the Hebrews and Latins disagree here', he says, 'but the Hebrews also disagree among themselves, since Rabbi Moses and Rabbi Solomon interpret and draw this differently.' Where there is no essential difference between Jewish and Christian interpretation, Nicholas gives only one diagram. The Bodleian owns a unique manuscript containing only the illustrations to Nicholas's *Postilla*, without the text (figure 71, MS. Laud Misc. 156, fols 5v–6r), which allows us to look at a number of the drawings side by side. Along with the contrasting figures of the menorah (top left), it also includes two curtains to cover different parts of the Tabernacle (bottom left), single drawings of the wooden boards of the Tabernacle (top right), and the High Priest, as well as two versions of the sacrificial altar, according to Peter Comestor and Rashi (middle right). Naturally, Nicholas too has a series of careful drawings of the Temple (figure 72, MS. Canon. Bibl. Lat. 70, fol. 165v), which includes the fire burning on the sacrificial altar, the menorah, and the stream (the river of paradise) running through the Temple compound.

This contribution is headed 'Imagining the Temple', but we must take care when we use the words 'imagine' or 'imagination' to understand properly what both Jewish and Christian commentators are trying to do. In common parlance, 'imaginary' is used to signal the antithesis of reality, suggesting that an author has employed creative licence to conjure up a picture which is at least a varnishing of the plain truth. But the Latin verb *imaginari*, which is how Nicholas of Lyra, for example, describes what is being done when he draws a picture, does not mean 'imagine' in this particular English sense. The Latin word is linked to the idea of 'likeness', and Latin 'imagination' is meant to produce as close a likeness as possible of the object imagined. In this sense, Nicholas and others are trying to use as little 'imagination' as they can, seeing the biblical text as a set of technical plans, to be followed to the letter, filling in gaps only as a last resort. Unfortunately, the biblical text is not as comprehensive as someone attempting such a practical reading would like, and some creativity generally proves necessary: the 'plain meaning' is not always in plain sight.

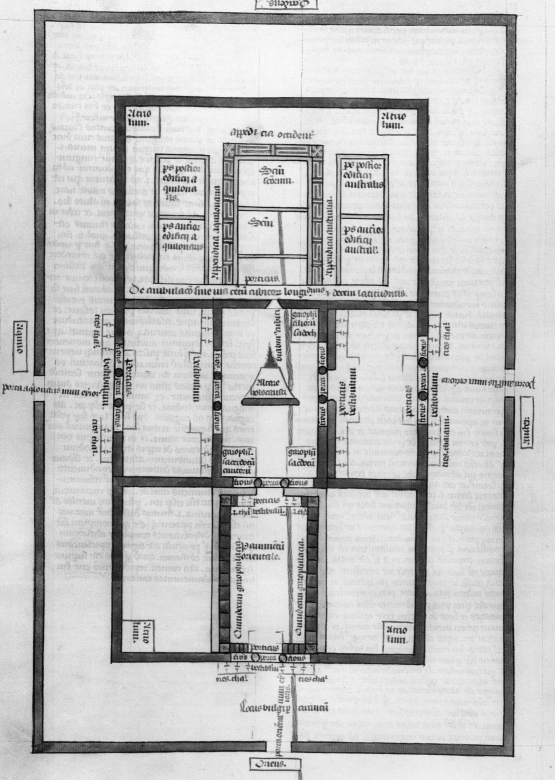

References

W. Cahn, 'Architecture and Exegesis: Richard of Saint-Victor's Ezekiel Commentary and its Illustrations', *Art Bulletin* 76 (1994), 53–68.

H. Hailperin, *Rashi and the Christian Scholars* (Pittsburgh, 1963).

P.D.W. Krey and L. Smith, *Nicholas of Lyra: The Senses of Scripture* (Leiden, Boston and Cologne, 2000).

H. Rosenau, *Vision of the Temple: the Image of the Temple of Jerusalem in Judaism and Christianity* (London, 1979).

K.L. Scott, *Tradition and Innovation in Later Medieval English Manuscripts* (London, 2007).

R. Wischnitzer, 'Maimonides' Drawings of the Temple', *Journal of Jewish Art* 1 (1974), 16–27.

CHAPTER 9

Christian Hebraism in Thirteenth-century England: The Evidence of Hebrew–Latin Manuscripts

Judith Olszowy-Schlanger

The fascination of Christian scholars for the *hebraica veritas*, the original Hebrew Bible, with its potential for the proper understanding of the divine message, goes back to patristic tradition, but receives its full expression in the course of the twelfth and thirteenth centuries. Conscious of the corrupt state of the manuscripts of Jerome's Latin translations, Christian scholars had been turning for instruction to their Jewish neighbours. Through learning sessions which must have resembled a mixture of a private tutorial and a polemical *disputatio*, Christian exegetes such as Andrew of Saint Victor in Paris learned about the Jewish interpretation of biblical passages.[1] This knowledge was conveyed to them orally, in French. Most of them never acquired more than a smattering of the Hebrew language, and their access to Hebrew texts depended entirely on their Jewish masters. By the mid-twelfth century, however, still with some assistance from Jewish teachers, several Christian scholars in England no longer totally dependent on oral instruction now turned their attention to the actual written Hebrew texts.

This shift from 'living sources' – Jewish teachers – to books implied sufficient mastering of the Hebrew language and grammar. Now texts and textbooks were acquired and, even more importantly, produced in order to facilitate access to Jewish literature. This language-oriented approach to Hebrew sources is represented in the twelfth century by such English scholars as Herbert of Bosham (*c.* 1120–1194),[2] Alexander Neckham (1157–1217),[3] Odo – a mysterious author of the *Ysagoge in theologiam*[4] or the anonymous Christian copyist of the bilingual Hebrew Latin Psalter from Canterbury (today MS. Leiden Or. 4725).[5] It reaches its peak in the following century, when a veritable school of Christian Hebraists produced a considerable number of manuscripts and their annotations referred not only to the Hebrew Bible but also

Figure 73

Book of Ezekiel (chapter 30) in Hebrew with Latin *superscriptio* and the Vulgate (England, early thirteenth century). Oxford, Bodleian Library, MS. Bodl. Or. 62, fol. 59r.

to post-biblical and medieval Jewish literature. The authors of these thirteenth-century works display an unprecedented knowledge of the Hebrew language and grammar based on a philological rather than polemical approach to rabbinic texts.

Since Beryl Smalley's pioneering work, this school of English Hebraists has been often associated with the Franciscans, mostly in the light of Roger Bacon's self-proclaimed role in promoting Hebrew studies, and his accounts of the involvement of Robert Grosseteste, bishop of Lincoln (*c.* 1175–1253), in the correction of the Latin Bible by reference to Hebrew. However, the Hebrew work actually attributed to Roger Bacon – one leaf of grammatical remarks in MS. Cambridge UL Ff.6.13 – is quite rudimentary, and shows a very inadequate knowledge of the language.[6] This work has no connection with the manuscripts produced by the school of English Hebraists in question. On the contrary, recent research on the thirteenth-century Hebrew–Latin manuscripts has identified different centres of Hebrew study in medieval England.

Indeed, contemporary with Roger Bacon, a group of anonymous English Christian Hebraists undertook the extraordinary task of systematically comparing the Hebrew text of the Bible with its Latin translations. In some ten manuscripts known today, this comparison is expressed by page layout consisting in copying the Hebrew text and its corresponding Latin translation in parallel columns. In most cases, to elaborate these unusual manuscripts, Christian and Jewish scribes worked together in close collaboration.[7] Drawing on Christian tradition going back to Origen's *Hexapla* and medieval *Psalterium triplex* with Jerome's various versions (Romana, Gallicana and Hebraica), the Hebrew–Latin bibles in parallel columns such as the Pentateuch and Psalter at Corpus Christi College, Oxford (MS. CCC 5 and MS. CCC 10) or the book of Ezekiel in MS. Bodl. Or. 62 function both as texts and as tools to study these texts. The perfect correspondence of the Hebrew and Latin verses and a clear and elegant presentation in well-planned facing blocks of text facilitate rapid orientation and matching of Hebrew and Latin words and grammatical structures. These bilingual manuscripts were carefully planned by means of a complicated pattern of ruled lines to guide the writing and to structure the bilingual page. This required some careful prior calculation: the Hebrew text takes on average half of the space required by Latin translation, since the vowels are written as a system of sub- and supra-linear dots and strokes and some prepositions and possessive pronouns are written as word affixes. In MS. Bodl. Or. 62 fol. 59r, there are, for example, seventeen written lines of Hebrew for thirty-one corresponding lines of Latin (figure 73). The individual Hebrew characters are twice as large as the Latin ones. The Hebrew text was written first and the Latin adjusted to it so that the verses begin on the same line. This technique of copying manuscripts with facing Hebrew and Latin texts was explained and given a deeper symbolic meaning in the anonymous preface to the Psalter MS. CCC 10, where the Hebrew text, written in an elaborate though not always successful chessboard layout, accompanies two Latin columns containing respectively Gallicana and Hebraica versions. The author, whom Beryl Smalley believed to be Robert Grosseteste himself, sees in the copying of two versions side by side a symbol of 'reconciliation of differences under the leadership of Christ' and an attempt to 'quiet the collision of two brothers in their mother's womb ..., lest, because they differ, they should always fight'.[8]

The correction of the Vulgate through the comparison of Hebrew and Latin texts went, however, much further than a simple critical apparatus. In thirteenth-century England, the Hebrew text was provided with a new Latin translation which followed not only the literal meaning of the Hebrew text of the Bible, but often proposed interpretations based on rabbinic commentaries and grammar books, chief among them the biblical exegesis of Rashi and the twelfth-century Hebrew dictionary of Solomon Ibn Parhon. This new Latin

Figure 74

Biblical chronology in Hebrew. Oxford, Bodleian Library, MS. Bodl. Or. 62, fols 1v–2r.

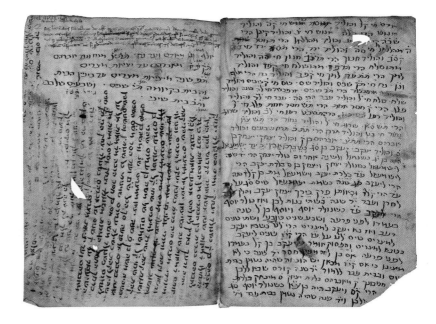

translation is written as a complete or partial gloss between the lines of the Hebrew text (*superscriptio*). It appears in some bilingual manuscripts (e.g. MS. CCC 5, MS. CCC 10, MS. Bodl. Or. 62), but also in Hebrew manuscripts written for Jewish usage which came to be studied by Christian scholars (e.g. Psalter MS. Longleat House 21, Psalter MS. Lambeth Palace 435). This *superscriptio* translation is referred to as 'ebreus' in medieval sources. It was again attributed by Beryl Smalley to Robert Grosseteste drawing on Henry de Cossey, who, in his *Expositio super psalmos* (1336), writes about a psalter in multiple columns belonging to the bishop of Lincoln as well as about his Hebrew psalter which he ordered to be provided with a *superscriptio* translation.[9] The authorship of the *superscriptio* is however less easy to ascertain: there are no less than seven psalters with a complete or partial *superscriptio* which varies from one manuscript to another (MS. CCC 10, MS. CCC 11a, MS. Cambridge, Trin. R. 8. 6, MS. Westminster Abbey 2, MS. Paris, BNF 113, MS. Longleat House 21 and MS. Lambeth Palace 435). There would have been therefore several different authors and origins of the *superscriptio*.[10]

One particular group of *superscriptio* manuscripts can be more accurately identified. MS. CCC 9 (Samuel and Chronicles), MS. Bodl. Or. 62 (Ezekiel), MS. Bodl. Or. 46 (Hagiographa), MS. Oxford St John's College 143 (Joshua, Judges, Canticle, Ecclesiastes), MS. Longleat House 21 (Psalter) and the Rashi's commentaries on Prophets and Hagiographa MS. CCC 6 all contain the *superscriptio* and marginal gloss handwritten by the same Christian scholar of the first half of the thirteenth century. They all use similar translation techniques and

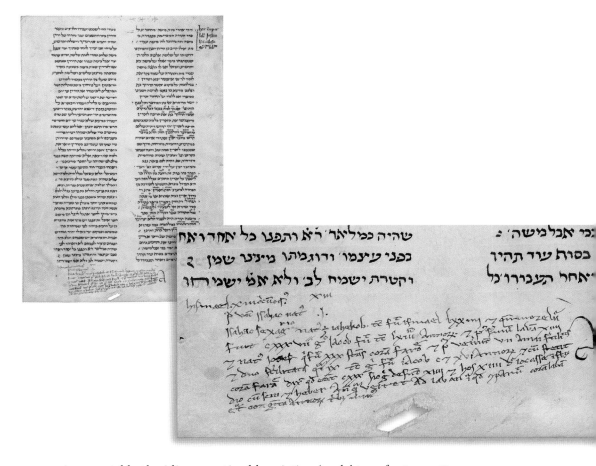

expressions, notably the idiosyncratic abbreviation 'enek.' to refer to the Aramaic versions of the Bible.[11] This scholar also used a specific simplified vocalization system which was common among twelfth and thirteenth-century Christians writing in Hebrew in England.[12] The connection between some of these manuscripts is further attested by the fact that a passage of a Hebrew work on biblical chronology copied on the flyleaves of MS. Bodl. Or. 62 (figure 74) was translated word by word into Latin and copied in the margin of MS. CCC 6 corresponding to the beginning of Joshua (figure 75).[13] As argued elsewhere, this group of manuscripts may be related to Ramsey Abbey in East Anglia.[14]

This 'Ramsey' group of *superscriptio* manuscripts served for a compilation which is probably the major achievement of the medieval school of English Hebraists: the MS. Longleat House 21: a trilingual Hebrew–Latin–Old French biblical dictionary (with some four Middle English words). This dictionary contains 3,682 separate alphabetical entries in Hebrew characters. These entries are transliterated in Latin characters, translated and illustrated by one or more Vulgate translations of the corresponding verses. When the Vulgate translation

Figure 75

Rashi's commentary on the book of Joshua. In the margin Latin translation of the biblical chronology found in MS. Bodl. Or. 62 (England, thirteenth century). Oxford, Corpus Christi College, MS. 6, fol. 1r.

Figure 76

Moses ibn Ezra's Glossary of *Sefer Tagnis* (North Campagne, France, thirteenth century). Oxford, Bodleian Library, MS. Bodl. Or. 135, fol. 233v.

does not correspond to the Hebrew original, a new translation is proposed. This translation is often referred to as 'ebreus', and is based either on a Jewish commentator (Rashi in more than five hundred cases), or on the literal meaning of the Hebrew text or again on the *superscriptio* Latin translation such as the one in the aforementioned glossed manuscripts. There is indeed clear similarity between the structure and the contents of many entries of the dictionary and the corresponding *superscriptio* and glosses in the Psalter MS. Longleat House 21, bound together with the dictionary and other *superscriptio* manuscripts containing various parts of the Bible. It seems that the dictionary itself was compiled and copied in Ramsey Abbey in East Anglia, where a group of Hebraists was active by the mid-thirteenth century. Their activities may be connected with Prior Gregory, known in later sources as Gregory of Huntington.[15]

While the origin of the dictionary itself in Ramsey can be argued on the basis of paleographical comparisons with other Latin manuscripts copied there, there are no indications that the related *superscriptio* manuscripts were also produced in Ramsey. However, since they were sources of the dictionary, it may be suggested that they were studied at Ramsey Abbey by the mid-thirteenth century. Furthermore, it may be possible to identify some of the manuscripts in question with Hebrew items listed in the early-fourteenth-century catalogue of Ramsey Library under the name of Gregory or his disciple Robert Dodeford.[16]

The philological approach was not limited to the Bible alone. The compilers of the trilingual dictionary quoted Rashi, as well as Aramaic targumim, Ibn Parhon, Menahem ben Saruq, the Talmud and, surprisingly, rare late narrative texts (aggadot) such as *Divrei ha-yamim shel Moshe Rabbenu* (as *Liber dierum Moses*), *Tales of Sendebar*, *Alpha Betha de-Ben Sira* and *Gamaliel* – the last an unidentified work often referred to in Christian sources, perhaps a Talmudic anthology.[17] Two manuscripts – MS. CCC 6 and MS. Bodl. Or. 135 – show that Christian scholars were indeed able to read these works. As stated before, Rashi's commentary in MS. CCC 6 belongs to the 'Ramsey' *superscriptio* group, and was quite probably the very book which was used to compile the Ramsey dictionary. In any case, it was diligently studied by at least three Christian scholars. One of them, whose handwriting is identical with that of other manuscripts of the group, provided several passages with a Latin *superscriptio* translation and marginalia of a philological nature (the commentary on Ezekiel in particular). As for MS. Bodl. Or. 135 (figure 76), an early-thirteenth-century compilation of various Hebrew linguistic and literary texts, its relationship with the 'Ramsey group' is unclear at present. It does contain annotations in thirteenth-century English hands which show that the Christian readers of this manuscript had studied the grammar of Ibn Parhon it contains as well as the Hebrew–Judaeo–French glossary of Moses Ibn Ezra's *Sefer Tagnis*, which was provided with interlinear Latin translations.

NOTES

1. See B. Smalley, *The Study of the Bible in the Middle Ages* (Notre Dame, Ind., 1983), 157.

2. See B. Smalley, 'A Commentary on the Hebraica by Herbert of Bosham', *Recherches de théologie ancienne et médiévale* 18 (1951), 29–65; R. Loewe, 'The Medieval Christian Hebraists of England: Herbert of Bosham and Earlier Scholars', *Transactions of the Jewish Historical Society of England* 17 (1953), 225–49; Loewe, 'Herbert of Bosham's Commentary on Jerome's Hebrew Psalter', *Biblica* 34 (1953), 44–77, 159–92, 275–98; E.S. De Visscher, *The Jewish-Christian Dialogue in Twelfth-Century Europe: Herbert of Bosham's Commentary on the Psalms*, Ph.D. thesis, University of Leeds, 2003; 'Closer to the Hebrew: Herbert of Bosham's Interpretation of Literal Exegesis', in I. van 't Spijker, ed., *The Multiple Meaning of Scripture: The Role of Exegesis in Early Christian and Medieval Culture* (Leiden, 2009), 249–72; D. L. Goodwin, *'Take Hold of the Robe of a Jew': Herbert of Bosham's Christian Hebraism* (Leiden, 2006).

3. See R.W. Hunt, *The Schools and the Cloister: The Life and Writings of Alexander Nequam (1157–1217)* (Oxford, 1984), 109; R. Loewe, 'Alexander Neckam's Knowledge of Hebrew', in W. Horbury, ed., *Hebrew Study from Ezra to Ben-Yehuda* (Edinburgh, 1999), 207–23.

4. H.G. von Mutius, *Die Hebräischen Bibelzitate beim Englischen Scholastiker Odo*, Judentum und Umwelt 78 (Frankfurt am Main, 2006).

5. See G. I. Lieftinck, 'The Psalterium Hebraicum from St. Augustine's Canterbury Rediscovered in the Scaliger Bequest at Leiden', *Transactions of the Cambridge Bibliographical Society* 2 (1955), 97–107.

6. S.A. Hirsch, ed., 'The Hebrew Grammar of Roger Bacon', in E. Nolan, ed., *The Greek Grammar of Roger Bacon* (Cambridge, 1902), 201–8.

7. On the bilingual manuscripts and discussions of the identity of their scribes, see R. Loewe, 'The Medieval Christian Hebraists of England: The Superscriptio Lincolniensis', *Hebrew Union College Annual* 28 (1957), 205–52; Loewe, 'Latin Superscriptio MSS on Portions of the Hebrew Bible other than the Psalter', *Journal of Jewish Studies* 9 (1958), 63–71; M. Beit-Arié, *The Valmadonna Pentateuch and the Problem of Pre-expulsion Anglo-Hebrew Manuscripts – MS. London, Valmadonna Trust Library 1: England (?), 1189* (London, 1985); J. Olszowy-Schlanger, *Les manuscrits hébreux dans l'Angleterre médiévale: étude historique et paléographique* (Paris, 2003).

8. Smalley, *The Study of the Bible*, 343–4.

9. B. Smalley, *Hebrew Scholarship among Christians in 13th century England as Illustrated by Some Hebrew-Latin Psalters*, Lectiones in Vetere Testamento et in Rebus Iudaicis 6 (London, 1939); Olszowy-Schlanger, *Les manuscrits hébreux*, 54–5.

10. Olszowy-Schlanger, *Les manuscrits hébreux*, 55.

11. For 'enek.' as a corrupted form of Onkelos, see J.-P. Rothschild, 'Enek.: targum araméen?', in J. Olszowy-Schlanger et al., *Dictionnaire hébreu–latin–français de la Bible hébraïque de l'Abbaye de Ramsey (XIIIe s.)* (Turnhout, 2008), lxxxi.

12. J. Olszowy-Schlanger, 'A Christian Tradition of Hebrew Vocalization in Medieval England', in G. Khan, ed., *Semitic Studies in Honour of Edward Ullendorf* (Leiden, 2005), 126–46.

13. J. Olszowy-Schlanger, 'Rachi en latin: les gloses latines dans un manuscrit du commentaire de Rachi et les études hébraïques parmi les chrétiens dans l'Angleterre médiévale', in R.-S. Sirat, ed., *Héritages de Rachi* (Paris, 2006), 137–50.

14. J. Olszowy-Schlanger, 'Provenance et histoire du dictionnaire', in Olszowy-Schlanger et al., *Dictionnaire hébreu–latin–français*, xvi–xxiii.

15. For the edition of the dictionary and its in-depth analysis and related bibliography, see Olszowy-Schlanger et al., *Dictionnaire hébreu–latin–français*.

16. For the edition of the Ramsey Catalogue, see R. Sharpe et al., *English Benedictine Libraries, The Shorter Catalogue*, Corpus of British Medieval Library Catalogues 4 (London, 1996) 336–9, 351–2.

17. Hunt, *The Schools and the Cloister*, 109; Loewe, 'Alexander Neckam's Knowledge of Hebrew', 214 n40; Goodwin, *Take Hold of the Robe of a Jew*, 139.

CHAPTER 10

Cross-religious Learning and Teaching: Hebraism in the Works of Herbert of Bosham and Contemporaries

Eva De Visscher

Hebraists whom we know by name and who have left writings that allow us to verify their knowledge in Hebrew are few in number. Perhaps the most famous are Hugh (d. 1141), Andrew (d. 1168) and Richard (1174), Augustinian canons regular at the School of St Victor, near Paris. While these men certainly display an interest in Hebrew and in Jewish thought, they probably did not know much beyond what could be borrowed from Jerome. Yet they consulted Jewish scholars independently, and can therefore be considered Hebraists in the wider sense of the word, even though their works do not suggest first-hand engagement or dialogue with rabbinic literature.[1]

With Herbert of Bosham (d. *c.* 1194) we are offered a very different picture, which may also be reflected in the work of Nicholas Manjacoria (d. 1145). A Cistercian monk at the Italian abbey of St Anastasius of Tre Fontane, Manjacoria set out to revise the Latin versions of the Psalms against the Masoretic Text of the Hebrew Bible. He consulted a Jew who introduced him to the work of the eleventh-century French rabbi Solomon ben Isaac of Troyes (Rashi). Manjacoria not only produced revised texts of the Psalms, but also a body of corrections on the Latin texts of the Psalms, and a treatise on textual criticism of the Bible. Since very little research has been done on these revised psalters, which remain unedited, it is impossible to determine what kind of Hebraist Manjacoria was, or the extent to which he borrows from Rashi.[2]

Herbert of Bosham shares an interest in literal exegesis with Hugh and Andrew of St Victor, and was familiar with their works. With Manjacoria, whose work he probably did not know, he shares the effort to revise the Psalms against the Masoretic Text, and to consult Rashi in the process. A flamboyant character and close friend of Thomas Becket, the archbishop of Canterbury, Bosham spent a large part of

Figure 77
Herbert of Bosham's
arrangement of Peter
Lombard's edition of the
Magna glosatura (England (?),
c. 1200). Oxford, Bodleian
Library, MS. Auct. E. inf.
6, fol. 78v.

his life embroiled in the political battle between the archbishop and
King Henry II. After the murder of Becket in 1170 he withdrew from
the political arena and lived in exile in France, where he devoted
himself to writing.[3]

Apart from two hagiographical works on Becket, Bosham produced two biblical commentaries. The first one, written *c.* 1173–77 is
the scrupulous arrangement of his former teacher Peter Lombard's
edition of the Great Gloss (*Magna glosatura*) on the Psalms and
the Epistles of Paul. The Great Gloss was an extensive ecclesiastical
commentary on the Bible, and an elaboration of an earlier version,
the Ordinary Gloss (*Glosa ordinaria*), arranged by Anselm of Laon
(d. 1117). Bosham's arrangement exists in only one lavish copy of four
volumes (Cambridge, Trinity College, MSS. B.5.4, (Psalms) 6 and 7
(Epistles) and Bodl. MS. Auct. E. inf. 6 (Psalter from Psalm 74 (75)
onwards, figure 77)). The books are dedicated to William, bishop of
Sens, and may have been produced there as well, before they ended up
at Canterbury Cathedral.[4] The volumes are magnificently executed,
and the layout is carefully organized, with the biblical text and main
commentary surrounded by two columns of cross references. The
notion of biblical commentary as a spiky dialogue or even dialectical
argument comes to the fore in the skilful illuminations which, where
not cut out, show Church Fathers vigorously pointing at comments
with pens looking like spears. Some even have a scroll coming out of
their mouths with portentous pronouncements such as 'I don't agree'
(*ego non approbo*).

Less apparent, but not less significant, is a series of neat corrections
made to the text of the Psalms. The Psalms appear in both Jerome's
translation from the Septuagint (called the *Gallicana*) and, in smaller
script, in his translation from the Hebrew (called the *Hebraica*). These
corrections, which occur mostly in the rendering of the *Hebraica*,
are in fact revisions against the Masoretic Text and correspond to
identical readings in Bosham's second scholarly work, a Psalter with
Commentary (*Psalterium cum commento*). Composed about twenty
years after the arrangement of the Gloss, this work consists of a
complete revision of the *Hebraica* and a commentary according to the
literal sense of Scripture.[5] It contains over a hundred Hebrew words
(all in Latin transliteration), makes extensive use of rabbinic scholarship, and displays a knowledge of Hebrew that surpasses that of any
known contemporary. The only extant copy of this commentary,
produced by a competent but not always careful scribe, is of English
origin and dates from *c.* 1220–40 (London, St Paul's Cathedral 2). It
is impossible to determine whether the corrections to the Psalms in
the Arrangement of Peter Lombard's Gloss were made *before* or *after*

aug.

de illis seductis fec̄. c c̄ e.

Et sublevabit pauperem de inopia: et posuit quasi greges familias.

Et adiuvit pauperem de inopia: et posuit sicut oves familias.

Et adiuvit illos pauperem: posuit illos deus patri semper inter. sed nos de illis non proficientes. Cum autem se pati per quoniam non indignetur, non nascitur in quo sit stultis studium: et timoris exemplum, ut qui stat videat ne cadat. sicut illi ceciderunt, qui sunt abiecti sunt superbi: et instructus est huius. quod ita dicitur. Et adiuvit pauperem de inopia, vel de mendicitate, id est qui se mendicum et inopem reputat, qui nichil sibi dat, sed totum de misericordia dei expectat, ante ianuam domini clamans et pulsans ut aperiatur ei. quem adiuvit plurimum de ipsa separatione hereticorum, quod fit in paupere adiuto de illis seductis multe familie. Unde subditur: et posuit illum pauperem familias. pauperem dico existentem: vel familias dico existentes sicut oves, propter simplicitatem et innocentiam. Lator: quasi unum pauperem putabas, sed iste pauper est multe familie, id est multe ecclesie. tamen et una est ecclesia: et una ovis. Vel ita. adiuvit pauperem: et per adiutum pauperem posuit familias sicut oves, id est servat familias in innocencia. Sed autem tanta mysteria dum latentia: videbit. [dicitur in] Sui etiam

Videbunt recti et letabuntur: et omnis iniquitas contrahet os suum.

Videbunt recti et letabuntur: et omnis iniquitas opilabit os suum.

Videbunt recti et letabuntur. Lator: quo psalmus tenuat ad hoc scilicet ut ostendat quod boni per misericordiam exaltantur: et mali per superbiam deiciuntur. Unde subditur: et omnis iniquitas garriens contra unitatem communem cum opilabit os suum.

Quis sapiens et custodiet hec: et intelliget misericordias domini.

Quis sapiens et custodiet hec: et intelliget misericordias domini.

Quis sapiens. Lator: conclusio psalmi. A. d. et qui pauperem adiuvat dominus: quis est sapiens et custodiet hec. scilicet ut sit pauper non dives. non superbus non inflatus. quis est sapiens? hec custodiet. et quia custodiet: id est qui intelliget, non in merita sua, non vires suas in his glorificando. sed misericordias domini. scilicet qui de errore liberat: et de consuetudine prava: et de tedio: et de naufragio. quoniam deinde constituit eum in prosperitate: non superbis resistit, sed humilibus dat gratiam. Intelligit: id est quod deus fecit ut inter manens multiplicetur: non foras eriens minuatur. hoc vident recti et letantur: et iniquus os suum opilat. Canticum psalmi ipsi david.

Para tum cor meum. In titulo: Canticum psalmi ipsi david. Iste est vi. psalmus de duabus naturis in christo. in plura eadem conveniunt. que supra in duobus aliis psalmis dicta sunt. que autem alia sunt parum differunt. Et posterius misericordia quam partibus duorum precedentium psalmorum. scilicet quinquagesimi secundi et quinquagesimi noni. quorum diversi sunt tituli: hic psalmus componitur. Nam postrema pars lvi psalmi: prima est pars huius psalmi: usque ad illum versum ubi dicitur: et super omnem terram gloria tua. Sed usque ad finem postrema pars est lix. Unde sciendum est titulos que de hystoria poni videntur: ex prophetia, id est spirituale intelligentia debere accipi: utrumque illum psalmum ad unum decurrere intellectum, non superficie hystorie: sed altitudine prophetie. copulatis partibus utriusque in isto psalmo cuius titulus neutri illorum est similis. nam quod hic et ipsi david: sicut ibi. Sed autem hic psalmus quem componit ex illis duobus: quorum tituli sunt diversi. intitulatur ipsi david. ut significetur quod multis partibus multisque modis olim deus locutus patribus in prophetis: tandem locutus est in filio, quem misit ut compleret eloquia prophetarum. et mirabiliter quod in diversis psalmis dicta sunt: in unum venerunt in hoc psalmo concrementa. ut quasi diversi sapores condiantur in pastum anime. unde licet et cantoribus adhuc tamen multa compinge. sicut et dicitur legitur in paralipomenon. c

Canticum psalmi david.

Paratum cor meum deus paratum cor meum: cantabo et psallam in gloria mea.

Paratum cor meum deus: cantabo et psallam in gloria mea.

aug.

aug.

aug.

aug.

aug.

aug.

aug.

v. i. multiphariam

this second commentary was written, or by whom, but it is tempting to imagine that Bosham, having improved his language skills and knowledge of Jewish exegesis over time, at some point made the corrections himself.

Considering the two works together, the reader is able to gain a remarkably vivid picture of the linguistic and exegetical development of a Christian scholar of Hebrew and of Jewish exegesis. In the first commentary, revisions against the Hebrew text are on the periphery, and the few Hebraist comments made are (literally) marginal. In the second one, Bosham, as previously budding Hebraist, has come into his own, and provides the reader with an absolute wealth of material, ranging from observations about Hebrew grammar and descriptions of text-critical devices of the Masoretic Text such as the *ketiv qere*, to views on the origins of Jewish festivals such as Purim and Shavuot. Before we can discuss his learning process and use of sources in context, three of his contemporaries (and compatriots) need further attention.

In the mid- to late twelfth century a certain Odo, otherwise unknown, composed a treatise titled *Ysagoge in theologiam* (Cambridge, Trinity College, MS. B.14.33). The work is a polemical one and has the express purpose of teaching the reader useful biblical quotations in Hebrew in order to refute the Jews in their own language – and possibly convert them. Recent research has shown that some of its Hebrew quotations display proto-Masoretic and even non-Masoretic features, and that their translations into Latin are on several occasions incorrect,[6] which casts doubt on Odo's level of Hebraism. Still, the occurrence of such a treatise does suggest that there must have been a Christian audience, however small, which would have been interested in as well as capable of reading it. Another interesting aspect to the manuscript is its use of the typical Christian Hebraist system of vowel-pointing, as analysed by Judith Olszowy-Schlanger.[7]

Ralph Niger (1140s–*c.* 1199) is a less obscure figure than Odo, and possibly knew Bosham. He, too, sided with Thomas Becket during the latter's conflict with the king. Because of his support for Henry II's sons in their rebellion against their father in 1173 he was forced to spend the rest of his life in exile in France. With the help of a Jewish convert called Philip, he wrote a Hebraist treatise which he titled after his teacher. The *Philippicus* is partly a text-critical correction of, and partly an addition to, different versions of a well-known work by Jerome, *A Book on the Interpretation of Hebrew Names*, a glossary of Hebrew biblical proper names.[8] His revision includes references to Jewish sources, which will be discussed below. Nothing of his exegetical oeuvre has been edited in full.

The same is true for Alexander Neckam or Nequam (1157–1217), who was, just like Odo, Bosham and Niger, a theologian of British origin who studied at Paris. Neckam taught at Oxford, and ended his life as abbot of the Augustinian house at Cirencester. At the turn of the thirteenth century he wrote a Gloss on the Psalms, based on the *Magna glosatura*, followed by a commentary on the Song of Songs in which he possibly includes independent Jewish material. Since these works have not yet been edited, and have been little studied, we cannot assess the extent of their Hebraism. What is known about them, however, reveals some intriguing nuggets of information which will be discussed below.[9]

How did a Christian scholar at that time set out to learn Hebrew, and what difficulties would he (we have no evidence of female Christian Hebraists) be likely to encounter? His own background and early education would have been a bilingual or even multilingual one. Christian children in twelfth- and thirteenth-century England spoke French or English at home. Latin was the language of formal instruction but, at least initially, French and English were used alongside Latin for translation purposes. Given the similarities between French, Latin and even English, which are all part of the same Indo-European language family, knowing the one language helped with the learning of the other. Hebrew, on the other hand, a Semitic language, would be a far harder nut to crack.

A first port of call with aspiring Christian Hebraists was the transliterated Hebrew material in the works of Jerome. This could be found in the prefaces to his Latin translation of the Hebrew Scriptures and in three treatises: the glossary of Hebrew biblical proper names mentioned earlier, a gazetteer of biblical place names, and a book titled *Hebrew Questions on Genesis.* Containing a mass of single words and phrases with often interesting, if not always correct, etymological explanations, they provided a useful resource for later authors.[10]

It would be difficult to overestimate the importance of the figure of Jerome in the minds of medieval biblical scholars, as translator of the Hebrew Scriptures, author of the standard Christian Hebraist reference works, and as authority on the basic principles of biblical scholarship. Bosham calls him 'the most learned examiner of the Hebrew language' and 'the foundation of all learning'.[11] From Jerome also originates the concept of 'Hebrew Truth' (*hebraica veritas*), the reading from the Hebrew text against which other translations have to be tested. *Hebraica veritas* became a well-known phrase among biblical scholars, and one which lent authority to later Hebraists' discussions of inconsistencies between the Latin text and its Hebrew source:

'The title of this psalm is usually *A Psalm of David, as or when his son Absalom was pursuing him*', Bosham states in his commentary on Psalm 142/143. 'However, according to the Hebrew Truth, the title is not like that at all, but rather *A Psalm of David*.'[12]

For Jerome, the process of learning Hebrew was a lonely one, and one fraught with difficulties. Systematic Hebrew dictionaries and grammars did not exist at the time and other Christians with an advanced level of Hebrew, from whom he could learn, were very scarce on the ground. This left him dependent on Jewish teachers whose knowledge he respected but of whose motives he was deeply distrustful, fearing that they would misrepresent the meaning of scripture because of their 'hatred of Christ'.[13]

Eight hundred years later Bosham uses the same rhetoric against Rashi, whom he calls 'untrustworthy' (*infidus*) on several occasions. Rashi and his followers tended to downplay messianic notions in the Psalms, sometimes explicitly 'as a retort to the Christians'.[14] 'Out of hatred for Christ', Bosham writes angrily, 'they have corrupted to these days ... what the blood of Christ has explained.'[15] Yet, as was the case with Jerome, Bosham is greatly reliant on Jewish sources, and the eagerness with which he absorbs these is by no means diminished by his ambivalence towards them – on the contrary, the former probably explains the latter. Interpreting these statements as 'the type of anti-Semitism prevalent at the time' would be too narrow. Rather, they form part of a virulent polemical debate between members of the two religions, beyond which we also find a rich cross-fertilization of ideas.

Bosham consulted at least one Jewish scholar whom he calls 'my grammarian' (*litterator meus*). *Litterator* can refer to both a teacher of reading and writing and a philologist, and the term occurs on almost every other page in Bosham's commentary, always indicating a Jewish source. Alexander Neckham uses the same term in the same way. He further offers us an interesting glimpse into the circumstances of rabbinic learning when he mentions that he has more than once heard the Jews discuss specific matters of biblical exegesis.[16] Since Neckham's writings do not demonstrate a sound knowledge of Hebrew, the language in which he communicated with the Jews must therefore be considered.

The Jews of England and France spoke French in their dealings with Christians and in daily life. Jewish children learnt their Torah with the aid of French translations. So-called *leazim*, French translations of obscure biblical words, occur frequently in rabbinic commentaries, such as Rashi's, and were compiled in glossaries for scholarly use.[17] It is of course entirely possible that Neckham could use the services of

Figure 78
Latin Psalter accompanied by the Hebrew text with Latin *superscriptio*. (England, 1230–1240). Oxford, Corpus Christi College, MS. 10, fol. 2r.

an interpreter when attending discussions on rabbinic exegesis, but it is more likely that enough French was used so as to allow him to understand what was going on without resorting to a mediator. Thus, for both Christians and Jews, multilingualism was the norm, and French, we might claim, a linguistic meeting-place for cross-religious learning.

Apart from the philological treatises by or attributed to Jerome, Christian Hebraists relied on three types of basic text and reference tool: the Masoretic Bible with Latin glosses and/or full Latin translation, glossaries or dictionaries, and grammars. (See the contribution by Olszowy-Schlanger in this volume.) Although most of these date from the thirteenth century, Bosham's Psalter with Commentary, written *c.* 1180–90, demonstrates similarities with some of them, such as the Longleat Psalter, the Longleat Dictionary and MS. CCC 10. With the latter Bosham shares countless identical readings which differ from the accepted Vulgate tradition. To give an example from MS. CCC 10, 2r (figure 78), both translate עדה, 'congregation', by *synagoga* instead of *congregatione* in Psalm 1:5, and have *narrabo* instead of *annunciabo* for אספרה, 'I will tell' in Psalm 2:7. This complex network of similarities suggests that the thirteenth-century bilingual bibles represent a well-established tradition of revising the Vulgate alongside the Masoretic Text, going back to at least the second half of the twelfth century and probably earlier.

As mentioned before, Rashi plays a huge role in Bosham's work, as borrowing source and as polemical opponent. Some of Bosham's comments are almost literal translations of passages from Rashi's commentary on the Psalms and he uses several of Rashi's *leazim* as basis for modifying the Vulgate text.[18] On one occasion, concerning the gender of ארץ 'earth' and תבל 'world' in Psalm 24 (23):1–2, Bosham

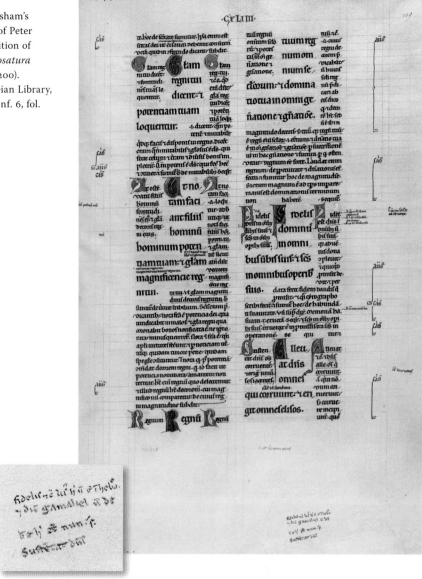

borrows an explanation from Rashi, citing as his source 'my gram-marian' (*litterator meus*). Whether he means to refer to Rashi or to his contemporary teacher is impossible to know but a gloss in the margin reads *Salomon*, Rashi's first name.[19] Overall, Bosham's interpretation of the 'literal sense' of Scripture has more in common with Rashi's 'plain sense' (*peshat*) than with other Christian literal commentaries of the period, such as those of Andrew of St Victor.

Another source, less frequently used but named several times, is *Gamaliel*. The word occurs in Ralph Niger's *Philippicus*, in Bosham's commentary on the Psalms, and as a marginal note in Bosham's earlier work, the arrangement of Peter Lombard's *Great Gloss* (MS. Auct. E. inf. 6, fol. 129r, figure 79). The note refers to Psalm 145 (144), which is arranged verse by verse, as an acrostic of the Hebrew alphabet, but lacks the verse for the letter *nun*. Yet the Septuagint and its translation, which list the Hebrew letters in transliterated form at the beginning of each verse, *do* supply the *nun*, followed by an extra verse.

'The Hebrew does not have this verse', the marginal note points out, 'and Gamaliel says that the *nun* does not belong here.'[20] It has been suggested that *Gamaliel* refers to the Talmud but it is more likely that it was a wider body of rabbinic source material, including Talmudic literature.[21]

Bosham also mentions and uses the *Mahberet*, a Hebrew lexicon by the tenth-century North African scholar Menahem ben Saruq. The word *Machuere* appears in Ralph Niger's *Philippicus* too, but mostly in conjunction with *Aruch*; it is therefore more likely that Niger refers to the *Mahberet arukh*, the grammatical treatise by Solomon Ibn Parhon (MS. Bodl. Or. 135, figure 80).[22]

Figure 80
Mahberet arukh, grammatical treatise by Solomon Ibn Parhon (North Campagne, France, thirteenth century). Oxford, Bodleian Library, MS. Bodl. Or. 135, fols 170v–171r.

Jews and Christians entertained views of each other that can be likened to a set of reflections on mirrors of different quality – on some mirrors, the image was only slightly changed; on other, it was deeply distorted. Similarly, in the works of the Christian Hebraists, we find reflections of Jewish scholarship, some rather vague, some featuring as target examples for polemical dispute, and some true to their source, to be assessed, argued with and integrated into Christian thought.[23]

NOTES

1.   R. Loewe, 'The Mediaeval Christian Hebraists of England: Herbert of Bosham and Earlier Scholars', *Transactions of the Jewish Historical Society of England* 17 (1953), 225–49 at 236; B. Smalley, *The Study of the Bible in the Middle Ages* (Notre Dame, Ind., 1983), 97–158; W. McKane, *Selected Christian Hebraists* (Cambridge, 1989), 42–75.

2.   J. van den Gheyn, 'Nicolas Maniacoria, correcteur de la Bible', *Revue biblique* 8 (1899), 289–95; A. Wilmart, 'Nicolas Manjacoria, Cistercien à Trois Fontaines', *Revue Bénédictine*

33 (1921), 136–43 at 136–8. V. Peri, 'Correctores immo corruptores: Un Saggio di Critica Testuale nella Roma del XII Secolo', *Italia Medievale et Umanistica* 20 (1977), 19–125; R. Weber, 'Deux préfaces au Psautier Dues à Nicolas Maniacoria', *Revue Bénédictine* 63 (1953), 3–17; Smalley, *The Study of the Bible*, 80.

3. On his life, see D.L. Goodwin, *Take Hold of the Robe of a Jew: Herbert of Bosham's Christian Hebraism* (Leiden, 2006), 9–50; on Victorine influence, see E. De Visscher, *Jewish–Christian Dialogue in Twelfth-Century Medieval Western Europe: The Hebrew and Latin Sources of Herbert of Bosham's Commentary on the Psalms*, Ph.D. thesis, 2004, 195–8.

4. C.F.R. De Hamel, 'Manuscripts of Herbert of Bosham', in A.C. de la Mare and B.C. Barker-Benfield, ed., *Manuscripts at Oxford: An Exhibition in Memory of Richard William Hunt (1908–1979)* (Oxford, 1980), 39–40; L. Smith, *Masters of the Sacred Page: Manuscripts of Theology in the Latin West to 1274*, Medieval Book Series 2 (Notre Dame, Ind., 2001), 45–8; P. Stirnemann, online review of Smith's *Masters of the Sacred Page*, *The Medieval Review*, 3 November 2002.

5. B. Smalley, 'A Commentary on the *Hebraica* by Herbert of Bosham', *Recherches de théologie ancienne et médiévale* 18 (1951), 29–65; R. Loewe, 'Herbert of Bosham's Commentary on Jerome's Hebrew Psalter', *Biblica* 34 (1953), 44–77, 159–92 and 275–98; Goodwin, *Take Hold of the Robe of a Jew*; De Visscher, *Jewish–Christian Dialogue*.

6. *Ysagoge in Theologiam*, ed. Arthur Landgraf, in *Écrits Théologiques de l' École d' Abélard*, Spicilegium Sacrum Lovaniense, 14 (Louvain, 1934); H.-G. von Mutius, *Die Hebräischen Bibelzitate beim Englischen Scholastiker Odo: Versuch einer Revaluation*, Judentum und Umwelt 78 (Frankfurt am Main, 2006).

7. J. Olszowy-Schlanger, 'A Christian Tradition of Hebrew Vocalization in Medieval England', in G. Khan, ed., *Semitic Studies in Honour of Edward Ullendorf* (Leiden, 2005), 126–46.

8. G.B. Flahiff, 'Ralph Niger: An Introduction to His Life and Works', *Mediaeval Studies* 2 (1940), 104–36.

9. R.W. Hunt, *The Schools and the Cloister: The Life and Writings of Alexander Nequam (1157–1217)*, ed. and rev. Margaret Gibson (Oxford, 1984); R. Loewe, 'Alexander Neckam's Knowledge of Hebrew', *Mediaeval and Renaissance Studies* 4 (1958), 17–34.

10. D. Brown, *Vir Trilingui: A Study in the Biblical Exegesis of Jerome* (Kampen, 1992), 11–24, 61–4.

11. *Psalterium cum commento*, London, St Paul's MS 2, fol. 5r: 'Hebraice lingue doctissimus inquisitor pater Ieronimus'; 2r 'tocius litterature fundamentum'.

12. *Psalterium cum commento*, fol. 155v: 'in quibus talis huius psalmi titulus esse solet *Psalmus David cum, uel quando, persequebatur eum filius suus Absalon*. Uerum secundum Hebraicam Veritatem titulus minime talis, sed *Psalmus David*'.

13. Brown, *Vir Trilingui*, 64.

14. *Rashi's Commentary on the Psalms*, ed. Mayer I. Gruber (Leiden, 2004); on Psalm 2:1, 177, 811; on Psalm 21:1, 253, 818.

15. *Psalterium cum commento*, fol. 18r 'quod Christi sanguis interpretatus odio Christi usque ad hos dies perverterunt'.

16. Hunt, *The Schools and the Cloister*, 96: 'Vix quicquam Hebreos audivi commodius exponere transitu isto'.

17. M. Banitt, 'L' Étude des glossaires bibliques des Juifs de France au Moyen Age. Méthode et application', *Proceedings of the Israel Academy of Sciences and Humanities* 2:10 (1967), 188–210; N. Golb, *The Jews in Medieval Normandy* (Cambridge, 1998), 176–95.

18. E. De Visscher, '"Closer to the Hebrew": Herbert of Bosham's Interpretation of Literal Exegesis', in I. van 't Spijker, ed., *The Multiple Meaning of Scripture: The Role of Exegesis in Early-Christian and Medieval Culture* (Leiden, 2009), 249–72.

19. Loewe, 'Herbert of Bosham's Commentary', 60.

20. Bodl. MS. Auct. E. inf. 6, fol. 129r: 'fidelis etc' versus hic non est in Hebreo et dicit Gamaliel non debet hic esse *nun*, scilicet 'sustentat Dominus'.

21. De Visscher, *Jewish–Christian Dialogue*, 158.

22. Loewe, 'The Mediaeval Christian Hebraists of England, 247.

23. O. Limor uses a similar metaphor concerning the Jewish and Christian self-image in the Middle Ages, *Bein Yehudim le-Notsrim*, vol. 5: Alilat ha-Dam (Tel Aviv, 1998), 49.

Index of Manuscripts